France

THE WORLD'S LANDSCAPES
Edited by Dr J. M. Houston

France

J. Beaujeu-Garnier
Professor of Geography at the Sorbonne

with a Foreword by

J. M. Houston
Principal of Regent College, Vancouver

Longman
London and New York

Longman Group Limited London

Associated companies, branches and representatives throughout the world

Published in the United States of America by Longman Inc., New York

First published 1975

Library of Congress Cataloging in Publication Data

Beaujeu-Garnier, Jacqueline.
France.

(The World's landscapes)
Bibliography: p.
Includes index.
1. Man — Influence on nature — France.   2. France — Description and travel.   I. Title.   II. Series.
GF571.B42   301.31'0944   75-28288
ISBN 0 582 48171 6 *cased*
ISBN 0 582 48178 3 *paper*

Set in IBM Baskerville 9 on 10pt
and printed in Great Britain by
Whitstable Litho Ltd, Kent

Contents

092   55856

List of figures

Foreword

by Dr J. M. Houston, Principal of Regent College, Vancouver

Despite the multitude of geographical books that deal with differing areas of the world, no series has before attempted to explain man's role in moulding and changing its diverse landscapes. At the most there are books that study individual areas in detail, but usually in language too technical for the general reader. It is the purpose of this series to take regional geographical studies to the frontiers of contemporary research on the making of the World's landscapes. This is being done by specialists, each in his own area, yet in non-technical language that should appeal to both the general reader and to the discerning student.

We are leaving behind us an age that has viewed Nature as an objective reality. Today, we are living in a more pragmatic, less idealistic age. The nouns of previous thought forms are the verbs of a new outlook. Pure thought is being replaced by the use of knowledge for a technological society, busily engaged in changing the face of the Earth. It is an age of operational thinking. The very functions of nature are being threatened by scientific take-overs, and it is not too fanciful to predict that the daily weather, the biological cycles of life processes, as well as the energy of the atom will become harnessed to human corporations. Thus it becomes imperative that all thoughtful citizens of our world today should know something of the changes man has already wrought in his physical habitat, and which, with accelerating power, he is now modifying.

Studies of man's impact on the landscapes of the Earth are expanding rapidly. They involve diverse disciplines such as Quaternary sciences, archaeology, history and anthropology, with subjects that range from pollen analysis to plant domestication, field systems, settlement patterns and industrial land use. But with his sense of place, and his sympathy for synthesis, the geographer is well placed to handle this diversity of data in a meaningful manner. The appraisal of landscape changes, how and when man has altered and re-moulded the surface of the Earth, is both pragmatic and interesting to a wide range of readers.

The concept of 'landscape' is of course both concrete and elusive. In its Anglo-Saxon origin, *landscipe* referred to some unit of area that was a natural entity, such as the lands of a tribe or of a feudal lord. It was only at the end of the sixteenth century that, through the influence of Dutch landscape painters, the word also acquired the idea of a unit of visual perceptions, of a view. In the German *landschaft*, both definitions have been maintained, a source of confusion and uncertainty in the use of the term. However, despite scholarly analysis of its ambiguity, the concept of landscape has increasing currency precisely because of its ambiguity. It refers to the total man—land complex in place and time, suggesting spatial interactions, and indicative of visual features that we can select, such as field and settlement patterns, set in the mosaics of relief, soils and vegetation. Thus the 'landscape' is the point of reference in the selection of widely ranging data. It is the tangible context of man's association with the Earth. It is the documentary evidence of the power of human perception to mould the resources of nature into human usage, a perception as varied as man's cultures. Today, the ideological attitudes of man are being more dramatically imprinted on the Earth than ever before, owing to technological capabilities.

To the geographer France has several significant connotations. It evokes visions of an extraordinary diversity of regions. It illustrates a remarkable interplay of historical heritage and culture, within their varied areas. It is one of the most humanized realms in the world, certainly of Europe. And French geographers themselves excel as synthesists of these realities, masters of evocative description and of a dual understanding of physical processes and human impact on landscapes. The writer of this work exemplifies the best of this geographical tradition of France. She also shows how a new France is in the making, the more remarkable in its transformation of landscapes because France was not affected by the Industrial Revolution as much as other countries of the West. It is now, however, in rapid change, and this study contributes an understanding of the scale and speed of this transformation.

J. M. HOUSTON

Part One

Factors of Diversity

Introduction:
The French landscape

The French territory represents only a tiny portion of the lands emerged from the sea and even of the European continent. Forty-four times smaller than the USSR and one-seventeenth the size of the United States, France nevertheless offers a vast range of landscapes, and its variety, proportionate to its area, is remarkable.

Everything contributes to this diversity.

The physical elements provide a changing framework. In this isthmus which links the north and the south of Europe and is attached to the continental land masses on the east while opening widely, like the outstretched palm of a hand, to the oceanic influences to the west, all the major zones of relief and climate broadly spread out in Europe, come together, and one can hardly travel more than 200 or 300 kilometres without seeing undulations in the relief and changes in the vegetation cover. By crossing the grain fields of the vast basins or the grassy and wooded ridges of the ancient rounded-off mountains one passes from the humid hills of the Armorican *bocage* (mixed woodland and pastureland) to the snowy mountain peaks of the south and southeast, or from the flat and foggy shores of the North Sea to the high, deeply incised rocks dazzling under the vivid Mediterranean light.

Moreover, in the midst of these changing landscapes, there live divers men whose ancestors have come time and again in the course of the millenia of prehistory or in the first centuries of our era, successively from the steppes of Central Asia, from the northern peninsulas, or from the southern shores. Originally contrasting types, these peoples mingled more or less completely. And each one brought with him his customs, his habits, sometimes agglutinating in dense villages or in cities with tall buildings closely crowded together, sometimes dispersing in rural hamlets far apart or in the long low streets of sprawled out towns. Some practised their agricultural activities in vast, open and deforested countrysides where nothing catches your eye; others sought the manifold shelter of hedges or of low walls, bordering precisely the majority of the fields. In the course of the centuries, rural and urban life evolved bringing many alterations to the initial themes, which still remain visible.

Scientific discoveries added increased technology to the vicissitudes of history. Little by little, man dominated more confidently his environment and imposed upon it many adjustments. The exploitation of mineral deposits, the progress of powerful industry, the continental modifications to means of communication, etc., gave France another dimension and fashioned for her another visage. Social preoccupations were mixed with economic undertakings, and the voluntary planning of the territory caused a more rigorous method of transformation of economic life and of the inhabited areas to follow the spontaneous achievements of free enterprise.

All these multiform influences, indissolubly mingled, are found in the French landscape today.

1
Variety of the natural elements

The French territory is profoundly affected by its location on the western perimeter of occidental Europe. It is, in a way, the résumé of the entire continent. A résumé of the relief, since we find the three major zones that stretch from east to west in continental Europe, tapered, brought together and closely imbricated: the vast, extensive northern plains, the backbone of ancient mountains in the centre, the Mediterranean world where young mountains are juxtaposed with narrow plains. Thus the territory's average altitude is 342 metres (greater than the European average of 297 metres), but this figure expresses the result of marked oppositions since 61.8 per cent of the territory is below 250 metres, while 6.8 per cent is over 1000 metres. In the vast area of plains and basins of the north and west, that is to say in three-fifths of France, the culminating point, the Mont des Avaloirs, reaches only 417 metres, while in the southeast, the average altitude of the French Alps, which contain the highest summit in Europe (Mont Blanc: 4807 metres), is 1121 metres. A résumé also of the climate with three sides widely opened, respectively to the oceanic influences in the north and west, to the continental influences from the east, and finally on the south is touched by the most northern advance of the Mediterranean.

All this announces an extraordinary variety. However, it is only by looking at a portrait of France, that is to say a map, whether of the relief, of the distribution of the underlying rocks or subsoils, the climatic types, or of the vegetation cover, that one realizes the extreme diversification of the territory and, in certain rather numerous cases what we can call a 'parallel diversification'. The large areas of plains and hills in the north and west, formed from sedimentary rocks, are open to oceanic influences, while the high mountains in the south and southeast offer the narrow southern plains the Mediterranean influences and protects them nearly completely from all others. Thus the French territory is first of all a mosaic of natural landscapes where the originality of each piece results from the wealth of combinations of the numerous physical elements.

The climatic conditions and their consequences

Three main climatic types predominate in France today: oceanic, continental, Mediterranean. The mountains, by their altitude, their

4

exposure, the shields that they form, introduce infinite variety to these types. Latitude also provides modification, but this is not very important as the maximum distance between north and south does not exceed 1000 kilometres.

The combinations of relief greatly favour the penetration of oceanic influences. Five thousand kilometres of ocean ramified along the coasts of the English Channel and the North Sea, swept by the westerly winds predominating at these latitudes, skirt the open plains rising gradually toward the east. Moisture and regularity are the natural gifts of this influence which predominates in its purest state in Britanny where the cool summer is hardly warmer than the mild winter (annual average variation of temperature at Brest is 10°C (50°F), with a January average of 7°C (45°F) and a July—August average of 17°C (63°F)), where it rains two days out of three, especially during the cooler seasons, where the winds blowing constantly push and break up the clouds at will. Grass and forests, particularly the beautiful oak forests, flourish magnificently under such conditions.

Along the coasts of the English Channel and especially along the North Sea, the winter is colder and the oceanic influences are lessened — the variation of temperature at Dunkirk is 13°C (55°F); the northerly winds are more frequent; the climate remains humid, the sky cloudy, but the summer is short and cooler. On the contrary, toward the south, the change in latitude is noticeable along the Aquitaine or Basque coast, particularly by the warmer summers, but the winter is colder, because the sea penetrates less than it does along the more indented northern coasts; the contrasts are more accentuated — temperature variation at Bordeaux is 16°C (61°F).

As one goes inland, the contrasts between the seasons become greater and the heart of the Paris basin, if during about two-thirds of the year it falls under the oceanic influences, also frequently falls under the continental influences to which the eastern part of France is largely bound. The alternation is particularly noticeable in the winter when the mild rainy days, which comprise the majority of the winter months often keeping flowers blooming in the gardens until December, are suddenly followed by dry, cold, sunny weather accompanied by the northern and easterly winds, which in a few nights reveal the rigorous winter of Central Europe.

The mountains all have the particularity of offering a terraced incline toward the west whether it be the regular slopes of the Central Massif or of the Vosges, the successive escarpments of the Pre-Alps and the Alps, the increasing height of the summits of the western Pyrenees. Thus it is the oceanic influences that dominate the greatest part of their extent, but the influences are lessened and rendered sharper by the altitude: the cold is accentuated, the moisture increases in impressive proportions. The northern Pre-Alps and the western Pyrenees receive the heaviest precipitation in France (2 to 3 metres of water). Snow replaces rain on the summits, and at more than 2700 metres in the Alps and 3000 metres in the Pyrenees, the snow is 'eternal'; snowfields and glaciers crown the summits of young mountains. All these zones of high relief constitute the precious water-towers from which flow the

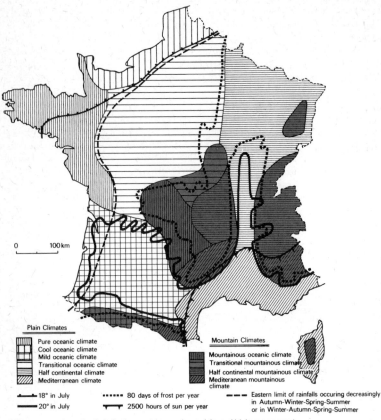

Plain Climates

	Pure oceanic climate
	Cool oceanic climate
	Mild oceanic climate
	Transitional oceanic climate
	Half continental climate
	Mediterranean climate

Mountain Climates

	Mountainous oceanic climate
	Transitional mountainous climate
	Half continental mountainous climate
	Mediteranean mountainous climate

⊢⊣ 18° in July   •••••• 80 days of frost per year   – – – Eastern limit of rainfalls occuring decreasingly in Autumn-Winter-Spring-Summer or in Winter-Autumn-Spring-Summer

⊢⊣ 20° in July   ⊤⊤ 2500 hours of sun per year

The mean annual quantity of rain for the mountainous regions and those which have pure oceanic climate is more than one metre per year

Fig. 1   Climate of France

majority of rivers having their source in France. Terraced on these long inclines, a whole range of vegetation types follow one another according to the altitude: crops occupy the lower slopes, and even vineyards on the *adret* (sunny slopes) of the least humid mountains; next come the grasslands, turning into the forested zones of oaks, beeches, conifers; beyond that, the heath (heather, broom, furze, and other thorny scrub) crowns the summits of the average size mountains, while in the high mountains these plants progressively disappear giving way to bare rock, and finally to eternal snow. Man has utilized all these possibilities and the traditional development of these mountain slopes has been one of the finest successes of the French peasant stockbreeders.

Beyond the summits, often situated on the culminating eastern border, the Vosges and the Central Massif drop down into corridors of plains, which are thus cut off from direct oceanic influences. Rather, these depressions open through the Rhine valley and the middle Rhône valley, toward Northern and Central Europe; from this comes a certain tendency for continental climate. Certainly, these areas do not experience the extreme contrasts of the Central European countries, but one does note, however, the brisk cold of winter and the heat of summer accompanied by storms, which give the heaviest rains of the year; the annual variation of temperature reaches 20°C (68°F) at Strasbourg, where it rains much less than at Brest, but a little more than in Paris.

These influences, which come from the continent, may go beyond the eastern borders of the country. In the winter, the anticyclonic air mass that covers Asia and extends into Central Europe, can invade the mountains and overflow into the French plains; in certain rare cases, it even reaches Brittany, thus blocking the way to oceanic influences, creating a pattern of calm, cold weather with clear skies and heavy frosts, which once every ten or fifteen years, destroy the mimosa in Brittany and the olive trees in Provence.

But the most original climate in all of France is that which characterizes the plains bordering the Mediterranean. The effects of the southern latitude are, in fact, reinforced here by two important elements:

1. The presence of an inland sea almost completely shut off from the ocean, aligned from east to west and bordered on its southern flank by the relatively hot lands of the African continent, and which brings as far as Southern France and Northern Italy the exceptional influences of heat and luminosity;
2. The mountainous frame of the Alps, Central Massif and Pyrenees, that comprises the three highest mountain units of France, shelters the Mediterranean influences and prevents the incursion towards the south of oceanic or northern air masses, except in the narrow corridors such as the gate of Narouze or the corridor of the Rhône valley.

The characteristics of the French Mediterranean climate are determined by this combined spread of Mediterranean influences and the shelter from the north: hot and dry summers and mild winters — apart from exceptional cold waves. The mean annual range of temperature at Nice is 16°C (61°F). Precipitation can be plentiful during the transitional seasons of spring and autumn; there is more rainfall at Nice than at Brest. But the rain falls in heavy storms with almost complete drought in summer, except for occasional showers. East of Toulon, it is not unusual to have three of four months with almost no rain during the whole summer. Exceptionally (about 65 days scattered throughout the year) a strong north wind blows along the Rhône valley, the famous *mistral*. The vine too, grows within this realm. On the uncultivated hills and plateaux desiccated by the summer drought, the thorny *maquis* of dense bushes (arbutus, heath, cistus, etc.) flourishes on the silicious soils, while the *garrigue* — long sparse vegetation — rosemary, lavender, graminaceae with some kermes oaks — occupies especially the calcareous rocks. The mountain slopes, more adequately watered, are covered with magnificent chestnut forests in areas such as the Cevennes and the Vivarais. On the plains, where the water is sufficiently abundant to permit well-developed irrigation, the climate is favourable for the cultivation of early fruits and vegetables.

The major types of landforms

To the north and west of the country extend plains, plateaux, and hills. Although vast open spaces, they in no way engender a sense of monotony. In the extreme northern portion of France is found the last ramification of the great Russian plain, prolonged by those which constitute the major portion of the Polish territory and a notable part of Germany and the Netherlands. Beyond the mouth of the Rhine, remains only a narrow segment which touches the Ardennes to the south and forms the northern part of Belgium, before fading away in France, at the foot of the hardly sketched out Artois hills (208 metres). South of the Artois ridge, the plains continue, but they are different. They are no longer uniform, undifferentiated with undulating and unorganized slopes; on the contrary, they are arranged in aureoles, in troughs, they converge between mountainous pillars which, even if they are of low elevation, like the Armorican Massif or the northern and western parts of the Central Massif, do add a certain stress, delineate gulfs of boundaries not too far from the sea, orientate the rivers toward the more or less ramified troughs which correspond to the central axes of the Seine, Loire, and Garonne valleys. To this more organized relief corresponds a different structure. The northern plain is made up of very recent sedimentary rocks, Tertiary and Quaternary, composed essentially of sand and clay, of which the recent dip — perhaps even still accentuated in historic times — toward the North Sea, is the essential characteristic.

The basins behave in another way. Here, everything (slopes, rivers) dip toward the centre. Recent deposits, Tertiary and Quaternary, fill only the central part, either in the form of thin layers of irregular hardness and sub-horizontal, as in the heart of the Paris basin where they give a terraced relief, that is little differentiated, or in the form of depositions that are more or less coarse, more or less thick, and constituted partly of marine deposits, partly of deposits of continental origin, as in the trough of the Loire and in the axial and southern parts of the Aquitaine basin, where plateaux and gentle hills have been carved out. Toward the periphery appear aureoles of asymmetrical relief, of *cuestas*, which follow one after the other up to the neighbouring mountains, supported by outcrops of hard secondary rock strata. These rock strata are arranged like gigantic basins; the rock strata become older as one moves away from the centre toward the periphery. The valleys follow the general dip of the relief and of the structure: they descend from the higher areas of the periphery, almost regularly toward the central trough in the case of the Loire or the Garonne, or else converge in a kind of central hollow, perhaps the origin of Paris fortune in the Paris basin.

Fragmenting and organizing these plains into basins, the mountainous backbone of the ancient massifs constitutes the skeleton of France. It is around these ancient stone protrusions that beat the seas responsible for the subsequent sedimentary deposits; it is from the debris of their erosion that are constituted the majority of layers which surround them; from their watersheds flow the rivers which diverge toward the greater part of the territory. Created in the Primary era, during the great convulsions of the Hercynian orogenesis, these ancient mountains of the Ardennes, the Vosges, the Central Massif and the Armorican Massif, have been worn down, reduced several times to the state of peneplains and then rejuvenated as a consequence of the Alpine folding during the Tertiary. The relics of peneplanation have been preserved in the monotonous plateaux or rounded summits, levelling the massive rocks of the mountain cores or the sedimentary rocks intensely folded during the Primary, while the rejuvenation during the Tertiary and Quaternary has left deeply incised valleys. The large fractured areas of subsidence opening up the northern part of the Central Massif or constituting the eastern boundaries of either the Vosges or the Central Massif, as well as the erupting and overflowing volcanoes, are further proof of this recent rejuvenation, that according to certain authors was prolonged until the Quaternary very close to historic times. In proximity to these Hercynian uplifts, as in the foothills of many contemporary mountain ranges in Western Europe, exist the great coal basins. The massiveness of their relief, rather than the boldness of their form which nowhere exceeds an altitude of 1900 metres, constitutes a barrier, from the point of view of climate as well as settlement, particularly in terms of establishing lines of communication. It strongly contributes to the division of the French territory in two parts: the north and the west turned toward the ocean, and the east and the south orientated toward the continent and the Mediterranean. The Rhône—Rhine link, which is one of the major themes in current French transportation policy, will express in economic terms this physical reality.

Indeed, at the foot of these rejuvenated escarpments, which border the ancient mountains to the east, a corridor of depressions stretch from the banks of the Mediterranean to the lower Rhine valley. Carved out either between two ancient mountain ranges, as in the Alsace area, between the Vosges and the Black Forest, or between an ancient massif and youthful mountain chains, as in the plains of the Doubs, the Saône and the Rhône, between the Jura and the Alps to the east and the Central Massif to the west, this corridor is still filled up with recent Tertiary and Quaternary formations, generally soft, more or less superficially covered with alluvial deposits forming several terraces. Its role as a corridor, in terms of climatic influences as well as for transportation, is remarkable, especially as it is ramified by passes and portions of valleys toward Switzerland, the western part of France, and the Paris basin. The fortune of Lyons is the result of this crossroads.

The territory's boundaries to the south and the southeast illustrate one of the fundamental tenets of French politics, whether under the monarchy or under the political regimes which have succeeded it, that is to say, the quest for natural boundaries. As a matter of fact, the boundary is drawn along the highest summits of young mountains, the Jura, the Alps, the Pyrenees; however, the coincidence between this physical fact and this political limit, was only acquired, in the case of the Alps, following the Second World War.

The only characteristic these 'young mountains' have in common is that they are relatively recent in comparison with the ancient central backbone, otherwise they are rather dissimilar. The Pyrenees are the oldest, already folded in the Secondary and again in the Tertiary; they embody a large axial zone, a portion of an ancient massif revived as a whole and raised to 3000 metres, giving this zone the character of a massive barrier and the weight of their elevated plateaux which provide a pedestal for their higher summits. They rise abruptly above the French incline that has been invaded by the mass of debris, eroded during periods of recent uplifting, outlining a vast cone of piedmont, furrowed by the divergent straight valleys. They decline in elevation only at the two extremities where they are naturally traversable, either through passes open throughout the year, or along the sea-shores. The Alps are quite different. More recent, more varied, more majestic, they descend steeply towards Italy, but offer France a long ascent up to the highest summits, exceeding 4000 metres and crowned by the giant of Europe, Mont Blanc. Few common traits, other than their comparable elevation, unite the northern Alps which are more regular, higher, and yet more open and better favoured, with the southern Alps which are tangled and not very accessible. On the fringe of the high mountains, where the central massifs also embody elements of the core raised to a great height, are found the Pre-Alps, made up of Secondary sedimentary rocks, strongly folded, faulted, pulled apart, carved out, a majestic relief that in a way the Jura prolongs, beyond the gorge cut by the middle Rhône. The Jura, a small Jurassic mountain chain, highest in the southeast, becomes progressively lower toward the west, and dominates the adjoining plains of the Saône with its calm plateaux. The Pre-Alps border the eastern part of the Rhône corridor that they cut off sometimes almost completely by advancing far enough to touch the foothills of the Central Massif. This explains the irregularities of the Rhône plains, sometimes opened out in triangular form, sometimes narrowed into gorges that the river cuts (Tain–Tournon, Donzères–Mondragon).

This then is the outline of the first lineaments of the physical framework: a compartmentalization of relief, based on a variable geology and shaped by a series of elements, the succession of which merits further consideration.

Stages in the formation of landforms

The oldest parts of the French territory can be traced to the Hercynian folding, the base composed of crystalline rocks, of Primary sedimentary rocks that have been violently folded, and of metamorphic rocks. The relations that exist among these three elements are complex: sometimes the Primary folded rocks cover the crystalline core, as in the Ardennes, sometimes they form gigantic folds, which determine the relief of present-day hills, as in the Armorican Massif; at other times they have been penetrated by the rise of further crystalline magma and have given the metamorphic rocks common in the Central Massif. The Hercynian folding erected these structures into mountains of considerable size: geologists estimate that they must have reached a height of 20 000 metres in the Limousin, today an area of calm plateaux. Indeed, the Hercynian chains have been worn down by long periods of erosion resulting first of all in what is called the post-Hercynian peneplain, a vast flattened area shaped over a long period of time, subsequently warped, and which we now see buried on the borders of the ancient massifs — sometimes under the Trias (sandstone of the northern and western Vosges), sometimes under the Lias and the Jurassic (north-western edge of the Central Massif), sometimes even under the Cretaceous (to the east of the Armorican Massif). The visible remains of this first stage are to this day considerable, since they constitute, in more or less altered form, the whole north-western part of France, the Central Massif, the Vosges, the Ardennes, and in addition one finds evidence of the same era in the considerably uplifted axes of the Pyrenees and the northern Alps.

Between these fragments of the core which have probably always existed above sea-level, have been hollowed out depressions, zones of repeated subsidence which have created either vast basins in aureoles (Paris basin, trough of the Loire region, Aquitaine basin), or narrow depressions, edged by geometric escarpments, filled up by the Secondary seas and subsisting imbedded in ancient mountains (Causses) or forming corridors between mountainous regions (Alsatian plains, plains of the Saône and Rhône). However, the abundant and varied sedimentation caused by the Secondary seas extended into many other areas. Certain people estimate that this sedimentation invaded even a portion of the peneplained core areas, from which it has now disappeared (Jurassic in the Vosges? Cretaceous around the Armorican Massif?); in any case, it widely buried the areas which subsequently were to become the theatre for the folding of young mountains, piling up thick layers of clays, limestones, sandstones, marls, sands, etc. And, from the Secondary on, we see the beginning of a new period of the Alpine folding, the Pyrenees were the first effected, soon followed by the zone of the central massifs corresponding to the most eastern and highest part of the Alps.

These movements developed in the Tertiary and acquired a considerable magnitude; according to certain geologists, their effects are still being felt. The Hercynian folding occurred about 220 million years ago; the Alpine folding began only about 60 million years ago. But since the dawn of the Tertiary there has taken place a series of events which profoundly marks the present-day world.

The most important is without any doubt the orogenic manifestations which, with the end of the first part of the Tertiary (Eocene—Oligocene) 'put an end to this sort of paleogeographic inversion by which the Tertiary chains presently the highest in elevation were occupied during the Secondary and the Eocene by the deepest regions of the greater Mediterranean. The late Tertiary seas now only pass round these mountain chains using the depressions that still border them today' (Gignoux, 1960). These folds which caused the different parts of the Pyrenees, the Alps, and the Jura to rise in successive convulsions, also influenced both the ancient massifs, and the great northern sedimentary basins.

According to the latest findings of French geologists, the phases of this fold can be followed in a very characteristic region, the northern Alps. A cross-section from west to east of this mountainous area shows four successive belts stretched out from the north—northeast to the south. To the west, the Pre-Alps, an intensely folded chain where the great limestone escarpments play an important role: the sub-Alpine trench is a series of depressions varying in width and form, separating the Pre-Alps from the central massifs stretching from the Arve valley (altitude 1000 metres at Chamonix) as far south as the Drac, passing through the crossroads of Grenoble (altitude 214 metres): the eastern slope of this sub-Alpine trench rests against the crystalline massifs, exceeding altitudes of 3000 and even 4000 metres in the ranges of Mont Blanc in the north and Pelvoux in the south, where eternal snow and glaciers crown the summits. Beyond, the internal zone constitutes a great arc and forms a divide; here lies the border between France and Italy, and the slope toward the Po valley is very steep. This internal zone is not homogeneous but includes powerful limestone massifs as the great Galibier, soft terrains eroded by the valleys (carboniferous, schist, slightly metamorphic glossy schist), hard and violent relief coinciding with highly metamorphic volcanic terrains like the green rocks of Viso (3841 metres), and the crystalline massif of the Grand Paradis (4061 metres). Across these parallel zones the valleys are often layed out perpendicularly southeast/northwest introducing a gridiron effect in the relief.

How can these forms be explained? In light of the most modern morphological and geological observations, Paul and Germaine Veyret proposed the following hypothesis, utilizing the theory of uplift and gravity flow. An ancient Hercynian chain, made up of crystalline rock, worn down and covered again by Secondary seas, was probably uplifted in the Oligocene producing internal crystalline massifs from which a cover of sedimentary rocks which had just formed then flowed toward the west, creating the first series of folds; these folds were presumably stopped toward the north by meeting the barrier of external crystalline massifs, while they spread out toward the south, utilizing the break between the Pelvoux massif and that of Argentera. About the same time, fierce erosion was attacking the new relief, and important deposits were forming in the peripheral seas. At that point occurred the uplift of the external crystalline massifs, creating the present-day high Alps, and in turn provoking a new sliding of the surface fragments toward the north and west. Thus the folded Pre-Alps formed, simpler on the west where they are autochthonal, more complicated in the northern part, where several folds of *nappes* cover one another. On the border between the external crystalline massifs and the *nappes*, a

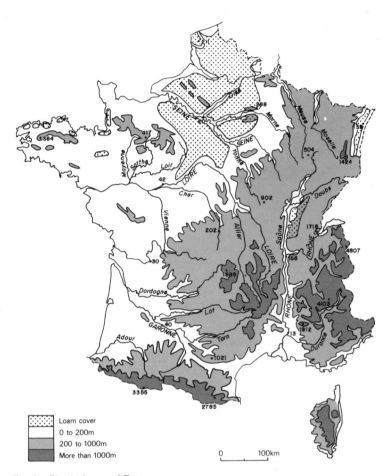

Fig. 2   Physical map of France

Legend:
- Loam cover
- 0 to 200m
- 200 to 1000m
- More than 1000m

0   100km

tectonic trench was produced which, was subsequently modified by different phases of erosion, producing the existing sub-Alpine trench. As far as the transverse valleys are concerned, they developed from the beginning in zones of weakness or morphological hiatus and they became more entrenched as the chains, which they now cross in impressive gorges (Arc, Isère, Romanche, etc.), were uplifted.

In the vicinity of these great Alpine folds, it was the Central Massif, among all the ancient French massifs, that felt the most serious after-effects, namely a violent uplift from the southeast and tilting toward the northwest, and, at the present time, it is the Cevennes which constitute the highest part of the ancient core. This uplift was accompanied by fractures, and beautiful fault escarpments of the ancient massif now

13

dominate the plains of the Saône and the Rhône, presenting a vigorous, rectilinear, well-demarcated edge, which contrasts with the hills rising progressively toward the high Alpine mountains. In these same Cevennes, the contrast is impressive between the ancient Hercynian peneplain more or less reshaped, rising progressively from west to east, and the jagged incisions caused by the attack of the Mediterranean torrents, leaving only narrow *serres* between them: from the belvedere of the Aigoual one can contemplate the contrast between two worlds, the Hercynian and the Alpine, and between two climates, the oceanic and the Mediterranean.

But it is not only the eastern edge which was overturned; the entire massif was uplifted and gorges were formed as far as the distant Limousin plateaux, showing the renewal of erosion caused by the uplifting of the core. In addition, fractures were produced inside the Massif: there are the fractures which accompany the Allier and Loire valleys in deeply sunken trenches, subsequently filled by Tertiary sediments and Quaternary alluvium (plains of Forez, of Roanne, Limagne). Accompanying these faults, was the appearance of volcanic activity, which has lasted from the Oligocene up to a quite recent era, since the last emissions from Parioux, in the Dômes chain, go back less than 8000 years. Certain edifices are considerable, such as the sharp Puy de Sancy, which at 1886 metres is the highest summit of the Central Massif, or the ejected mass of the Cantal; sometimes, veritable needles rise above the plateau of the ancient core (Mézenc, Gerbier de Jonc where the Loire has its source), while volcanic flows produce some famous geometric forms (such as the *Orgues d'Espaly* (Organs of Espaly), near the peaks of Puy en Velay, and the *Orgues de Bort*). Thus the relief of the Central Massif was upset at this time, and it is rather difficult to refer to the area as 'old mountains' unless the epithet 'rejuvenated' is added.

The same is true for the Vosges, also uplifted from the southeast and fractured on the Alsatian border in the series of steps whose present height was probably still being increased up to the beginning of the Quaternary. On the contrary, the Ardennes and the Armorican Massif were only uplifted, and the subsequent erosion created deeply entrenched river valleys or emphasized the crests of hard rocks, the sharp thin strips of vertical quartzites, which constitute the famous Appalachian relief, having the highest summits in northern Brittany (Monts d'Arrée: 384 metres).

Finally, in the depressed zones, the advance of Tertiary seas took place largely in the Paleogene (first part of the Tertiary) in the Parisian gulf and in the gulf of Aquitaine, and more sporadically in the small Breton gulfs; as the Tertiary advanced, the sedimentation was narrowed to lakes in the central part of the Paris basin, while in the eastern part of Brittany and Aquitaine, the Atlantic thrust broad advances. Among others the famous Sea of the Faluns, which began in the Cotentin region, covered over the areas of Rennes and Angers, and extended as far as Tours, Blois, and Chinon, was succeeded by the Redonian Gulf, which, still covering over the Angers region, extended toward Redon and Nantes; this subsidence of the west led to the modification of the course of the Loire, which previously flowed into the centre of the Paris basin, and now found itself diverted toward the Atlantic.

Throughout the periods of sedimentation, the basins also felt the attenuated effects of anterior or contemporary folds. This accounts for the northwest—southeast undulations in the Secondary and Tertiary terrains of the Paris basin, which undoubtedly were formed over several periods, because the axes of the chalk folds do not exactly coincide with those smaller Tertiary folds. In any case, these manifestations have visible consequences on the current landscape: the general orientation of the Seine valley, from above Paris as far as the sea, the orientation of the anticlinal hills of Bray and of Artois more or less cut away by erosion, and the orientation of the Somme valley. These are all regularly orientated from the southeast to the northwest under the influence of the axes of these folds.

However, the Tertiary was not only a period of movement; on the ancient core areas as on the sedimentary terrains which had just been deposited, a series of erosion surfaces, of fragmentary peneplains, developed. On the ancient massifs we could speak of 'polygenic peneplains': the Limousin plateaux, the crystalline core of the Central Massif beneath the volcanic relief formed later, the plateaux of the Ardennes, of the Armorican Massif, all reveal prolonged, recurrent periods of erosion. Certain authors have spoken of the 'Tertiary rock sickness'. Indeed, several times during the course of this geologic period, the French territory experienced alternating climates (humid alternative with hot and arid), similar to those of tropical Africa today, which favoured the decomposition of crystalline rocks by weathering of the feldspars. From this result piles of quartzose sands, that one encounters accumulated on the surface of the peripheral plateaux of the ancient massifs (Périgord, Sologne), and which permit the growth on the calcareous plateaux of forests and sandy moors, analagous to those of the acid crystalline terrains of the massifs. The same phenomenon is responsible for the deposits of kaolin which created and made famous the porcelain of Limoges. On the sedimentary terrains, the weathering was just as important: enormous thicknesses of chalk were thus decomposed producing the famous clay flint that covers a part of the chalky plateaux of northern France, rendering them impermeable and propitious to pasture (eastern Normandy). Finally, the calcareous surfaces which outcropped at this period, particularly those of the Tertiary limestones in the centre of the Paris basin, were weathered by *meuliérisation*, a process which created caverns with the dissolution of the limestone and made them extremely hard and impermeable with the penetration of silica. Such formations serve literally as protective coverings over the *buttes* of the Paris basin and assure their conservation.

All these Tertiary events occurred simultaneously: the mountains uplifting, the sedimentation continuing in the lowest portions of the basins, while in the intermediate slopes were formed more or less extensive erosion surfaces. The study of these surfaces has very much preoccupied French geographers and two schools of thought developed. The first following William M. Davis and Emmanuel de Martonne, was represented for a long time by Henri Baulig and based its explanation on the theory of interlocking cycles. Thus the Limousin, which presents, from the periphery toward the centre, a series of plateaux in steps whose most remarkable tiers are situated around 350—400 metres, 600 metres and 900 metres, has been presented by Demangeon (1910, 20) and Perpillou (1940) as the result of three successive erosion cycles, acting on a block uplifted in jerks; the earliest period having shaped the surface which is now found at the summit, and the most recent periods having successively cut the two peripheral rings. On the contrary, the 'mobilist' geographers like Beaujeu-Garnier (1954, 269) and Bomer (1954, 165), consider the Limousin as a block dislocated several times in the course of the Tertiary; its escarpments are not interpreted as the separation between two successive erosion cycles but correspond rather to differential erosion or to the trace of tectonic fractures; finally climatic erosion played a big part in shaping the surfaces by the deterioration of rocks, cleared away afterwards at the time of climatic changes. The second hypothesis comes much closer to reality and is confirmed by the verification of certain accidents of the Hercynian era repeated in contemporary times in the northern part of the Central Massif.

This simple example shows how very difficult it is to take a position in the midst of multiple explanations and differing dates which have been proposed for the major elements of plateaux or the most visible escarpments which characterize a large part of France's relief at the present time. Thus Cholley (1956; 1960) and Tricart (1948—52), among others, have clearly shown the importance of Tertiary surfaces in shaping the rings of plateaux which constitute the east and centre of the Paris basin and in the laying out of the drainage network: the rivers having been laid down on a surface regularly inclined from the periphery toward the centre and then having been embanked where they were in the hard layers forming the relief of asymmetrical *cuestas* that one crosses going from the Brie region toward the Vosges.

However, still another stage was to bring other upheavals in the periods of formation of the French territory. It was the Quaternary. If this last geological era, with its 200 000 years, appears as a mere instant in contrast to the 54 million years of the Tertiary era, to the 135 million years of the Secondary era, and even more so to the 360 million years of the Primary era, its role in making the details of the morphology has nevertheless been determinant. Indeed, in the course of these last millenia profound variations in climate have succeeded one another, bringing an appreciable drop in temperature in Europe and expressing itself by the existence of cyclic glacial periods. The exact number of glacial periods and inter-glacial cycles is disputed. In any case, the latter have an importance expressed in a variety of ways. One of the most recent interpretations is shown in Table 1.1.

Though the entire French territory was not touched by the glaciations, as were for example the Scandinavian territory or the major part of the territory of the British Isles, nevertheless important ice-caps rested on the great Alpine or Pyrenean chains, while local glaciers existed around the Cantal in the Central Massif, in the southern Vosges,

Table 1.1   Quaternary events

Alpine glaciations	Date	Climate	Sea-level changes	Human settlement
			Dunkirk transgression + 5 m	Historic period
Post Würm	*c.* 8000	Temperate	Flandrian transgression + 15 m	Neolithic Mesolithic
Würm	*c.* 90 000	Cold	Pre-Flandrian regression	Magdalenian; Solutrean; Aurignacian
Inter-Riss-Würm		Temperate	Monastirian transgression	Mousterian
Riss	*c.* 200 000	Cold	Regression	Levalloisian Acheulean
Inter-Mindel-Riss		Warm	Transgression	
Mindel	*c.* 500 000	Cold	Regression	
Inter-glacial		Temperate Warm	Transgression	Abbevillian Chellean
Gunz	*c.* 600 000	Cold		

and in Corsica. Around these localized glaciations and between glacial periods prevailed a climate qualified as 'periglacial' and whose importance has also been very great. The consequences of the glaciations and their sudden changes are responsible for many of the surface features effecting cultivation, communications, and human life in general. The large glaciers carved out in the northern Alps large U-shaped valleys propitious to communication and to human settlement. This is the reason why roads, railways, factories and entire cities could be established in the heart of the mountains, and why Grenoble, capital of the French Alps, and the largest city in the European Alps can lodge in the mountains, its 332 000 inhabitants at an altitude of 214 metres; for the same reason one can circulate easily at the foot of Mont Blanc, where Chamonix is at an altitude of 1100 metres. These great excavations, often still occupied by lakes, have also attracted tourists into the Vosges, Lakes Gérardmer, Retournemer, Longemer, as also to the northern Pre-Alps Annecy, Aix, etc. When the glaciers melted, the water thus released increased the flow of all the rivers thereby creating the large valleys in which their current heirs meagerly meander. Thus exist the large valleys in the centre of the Paris basin, where cities can easily develop along the banks of the Seine, the Marne and the Oise, whose broad floodplains are surprising considering the volume of water that flows in these rivers at the present time.

Around the glaciers and after their disappearance, the periglacial

17

climate which prevailed favoured the weathering of hard rocks, the soil creeping by solifluction of clayey debris. As a consequence, ancient valleys in the high mountains were filled up: this was the case in the Limousin highlands where valleys rendered 'senile' by such flows have practically disappeared from the landscape; other examples of this are the *ouches* (valleys in which the sandy deposits have filled the bottom) of the Morvan, the peat-bogs. . . . Asymmetrical slopes such as in the north—south valleys of the Armagnac hills where the eastern slopes are covered with solifluction deposits, while the opposite ones are steeper, are a further evidence of the existence of this periglacial climate. During this same period, strong winds removed dust particles from certain areas and accumulated them elsewhere in the form of fertile lime which enriched the chalk plateaux of Picardy, the limestone of the Beauce, the alluviums of Limagne, or even of the loess which enriches the high terraces of the Alsatian plains. To evaluate the importance of these facts, it suffices to contrast the richness of the alluvial soils of Picardy with the poverty of the bare chalk of Champagne, the majestic, regular aeration of the northern Alps with the almost untraversable confusion of their sisters to the south that the glaciers have not carved out. While twenty or thirty years ago geomorphologists tended to consider that the physical landscape was the inheritance of extremely old geologic periods, current scholars think that a large part of the physical features of the French territory and, among these features, many of those which are most important in man's daily life, are linked to very recent evolution, in large part Tertiary and Quaternary.

However, the great climatic fluctuations were accompanied by changes in sea-level (see Table 1.1, p. 17) and — whatever were the causes upon which specialists do not agree — this is responsible for important facts. First of all the shaping of large valleys along which we find a series of terraces. There again a conflict exists between the adherents of cyclic theories and the adherents of 'mobilist' theories. The former recognize the banks of terraces that are found in certain places along the courses of the large rivers of occidental Europe, and in particular along the Seine and the Loire, as the successive stages of the incision of the large rivers (90—100 m; 55—60 m; 35—40 m; 15—20 m); the highest terraces would be the oldest, and they would be related to the glaciations and the variations in sea-level. However, the improbability of this simplistic theory has been proved for a long time: the different altitudes of this type signify nothing, and to explain these forms, which undeniably exist in certain places, it is necessary rather to summon more complex and more localized facts, associating variations in levels, climatic fluctuations, and regional accidents.

The same holds true for the physiognomy of the shorelines. There too, for a long time people tended to see in the terracing, the pure and simple expression of former relative altitudes reached by the ocean waters. At the present time, here too, the 'mobilist' theory has taken on great importance. It is none the less true that, on the Breton coasts, for example, Guilcher (1948) was able to show the relationship between periods of marine transgression and regression in certain details of the coastal relief. Thus, Mont-Saint-Michel became an island and the deep

Breton rias were invaded by the sea only during the last known marine transgressions.

Thus we can say that, in France, the geological history of the end of the Quaternary intermingles with that of the first human settlements and the consequences of human settlement mingle in turn with those of the natural environment.

2
The human grasp

Within this general framework of diverse physical environments, man has exerted a long influence in numerous ways, at times extremely dependent upon natural conditions and at other times, for political or technical reasons, extremely independent. Twenty centuries of recorded history (and how many years of plodding along during prehistoric times?) have little by little fashioned for France a new face: clearing the forests, planting the most diverse crops and the most dissimilar villages and cities. Man has profoundly imposed his mark. There are no French regions where man has not left traces of his passage, no place where he has not ventured, and very few places that he has not transformed several times according to his needs or his possibilities. In the course of these last years was celebrated the two-thousandth anniversary of cities like Paris and Lyons, but we could go back perhaps two or three times farther to explain certain characteristics of rural landscapes, certain implantations of human communities. And inversely, at the present time new cities are created practically every year in France, evidencing a permanence and a renewal which is the appendage of almost all the old European countries. Indeed France is in the human domain likewise, a veritable microcosm of European features.

Millenia of vicissitudes

A crossroads, an 'end of the world', is evidenced by the name given to the tip of Brittany — the 'Finistère' — for the men who lived up until the end of the fifteenth century. Before the discovery of the New World, France found herself placed both at the point of convergence and termination for the great flows coming from the east. It is a fact that the majority of the great human migrations, since prehistoric times where we begin to pick up the traces, seem to have had a marked predilection for the 'conquest of the west' across the continents of the Old World. In any case, as far as France is concerned, the fact is striking; the territory has recorded the consequences of its position during the course of the millenia by the different stages of settlement and resource development.

Prehistory
From prehistoric times, we can distinguish the contributions brought from the most diverse areas; each of them introduced elements whose

traces certain historians enjoy finding in the details of present-day life. 'Our modern world was created five millenia ago' according to the witticism cited by René-Louis Nougier (1959).

France was, in the Stone Age, the theatre of civilizations which have left more developed remains here than have been found elsewhere in Europe; thus, it is not surprising that, except for the Clactonian, whose name comes from the English site, all the names from this period are linked with French sites. As far back as 500 000 years B.C., the Pithecanthropes left traces both in the Somme valley (Abbevillian) and in the Marne (Chellean); then during subsequent periods, sites multiply and technology changes. A map of the discoveries made in France shows the importance of the valleys of the Somme, the middle and lower Seine, the Charente, and the Dordogne where, in the rock shelters near Les Eyzies, the Paleolithic population reveals a surprising density; the caves of the central Pyrenees are reoccupied on several occasions millenia apart; later settlements penetrate the northern valleys of the Central Massif and densely occupy the Ardèche valley. Already the major mountain folds and the major valleys seem to be barriers, frontiers between distinct civilizations; human settlement, despite the 'Magdalenian explosion' and the flourishing of improving technology, remains very discontinuous. One of the most densely and most continuously populated regions was the Atlantic zone between the Loire and the Garonne, climatically privileged during the glaciations because it was situated far from both the great northern ice-caps and the secondary ice-caps covering the highest mountains.

In this privileged area between the two rivers 'all the Upper Paleolithic civilizations are represented' and 'of the 400 Magdalenian sites recorded in France, 300 are found in the southwest'. Curiously, however, the end of the glacial periods (*c*. 10 000 B.C.) is also the termination of this first period of human expansion. Undoubtedly, the development of the forest, under a humid climate, dealt a blow to these hunting and fishing societies better adapted to the bareness of the steppes associated with the former glacial climates.

It is not until the Neolithic that we see the resumption and affirmation in France of the great tradition of prehistoric settlement, active and ingenious, after an eclipse of several millenia. About 4000 B.C. two groups of people take root in France, one coming from the area of the Danube through Central Europe and the valleys of the northeast, and the other from the eastern Mediterranean via the shores of south-eastern France. By the Middle Neolithic (*c*. 3200 B.C.) the French territory is largely occupied. The domestication of animals supplements hunting and fishing, while cultivation makes its appearance and the phenomena of sedentary occupation are noted. Without dwelling too long on these obscure origins, at least one well-studied culture should be mentioned, for example that of the *Campigniens**, people of the Middle Stone Age who came from the northeast; a sedentary people, cultivating cereals, their settlement area can be delimited by the valleys of the Meuse,

---

* Campigny: a *butte* in the commune of Blangy-sur-Bresle, in the region of the lower-Seine.

Sambre, Oise, Seine and Loire. They helped fight against the invasion of the forests, corresponding to a wetter climate. Armed with the 'flint-axe hewed on both ends with a large sharp cutting edge', an efficient method for clearing trees, these *Campigniens* settled the first peasants along the edges of the plateaux 'not losing sight of the valley which brings water and the complementary resources of its forested slopes' (Nougier, 1959). Thus, without a doubt, their settlement helped protect certain regions like the Beauce, for example, from invasion by the forest. The plateaux of large-scale farming in the Paris region became subject to sedentary cultivation from this point on, that is to say 4000 to 5000 years B.C.

In the Mediterranean lands 'the struggle against the forest began much later, during the third millenium B.C., when the combat with the forest was won in the north, and ended by the retreat of the forest approximately to its present-day limits. The *Campignien* axe was largely responsible for clearing the forests in the north during the fifth and fourth millenia B.C. In the south, during the third, fires prepared the pasture lands for sheep and goats' (Nougier, 1959). At the end of the third millenium B.C., the Chalcolithic and Bronze periods are characterized by important transportation phenomena. Commercial routes appear, that can be traced by the stone relicts shaped like chalices, that are found in the southeast, the Paris region, the Armorican Massif, the western part of Vendée, the south-western Pyrenees . . . 4500 dolmens, at least, attest the importance of settlement and activity in France during this period. A little later, men of the Iron Age also pushed west from Central Europe: men from Hallstadt in the first millenium B.C., then those from La Tène, representing the Celtic civilization, that the Roman conquest overran in Gaul. It was believed that certain rural landscapes could be attributed to these civilizations, particularly in Bugey, the eastern part of the Paris basin and the Armorican lands. Some have even wanted to attribute certain fundamental antithetical traits of agrarian landscapes, which as yet have not been satisfactorily explained, to the establishment of one or the other of those primitive human communities. Thus the contrast between the openfield and the *bocage* or between dispersed and agglomerated settlements, for example, has been explained sometimes, locally and in terms of specific details, by this heritage of prehistory or protohistory.

The Gallo-Roman period

It is in France that there opened a new era, that of *pax romana*, after the defeat of Vercingetorix at Alesia in 52 B.C.; a country penetrated several times by the waves of civilizing invasions from the Germanic world, already grouped in *cités** respecting rather closely the natural divisions (as the historian Juillan (1903) noted: 'the appearance of the land changes precisely on the spot where the limit of the Gallic *cité* was found. When on the road from Orleans to Paris, one leaves the eternal and dull wheat fields of the Beauce and enters the graceful and

---

* The word *cité* designates here the area occupied by a certain type of population, a 'tribe'.

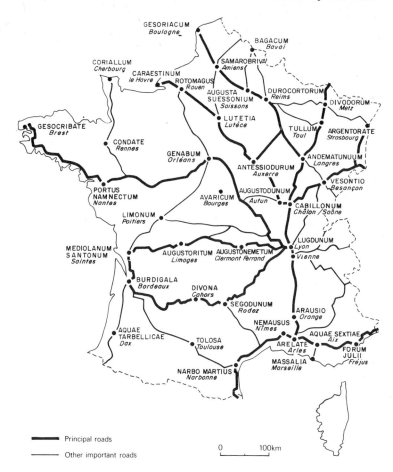

Fig. 3   Gaul in the time of Roman domination (cf. Fig. 8, p. 75)

picturesque valleys of the Etampes basin, one passes at the same time from the *cité* of the Carnutes into that of the Parisians'), inhabited by industrious people, renowned for their manual skill and for their virtuosity in metal work, but not very united, poorly organized, undisciplined. The Romans united under one rule southern Gaul, romanized since 121 B.C., with northern and central Gaul, until then independent and divided. This began what can be called the 'romanization' which was to last approximately four centuries and determine many of the features of present-day France.

Divided into four provinces, provided with a centralized administration with Lyons as its capital, Gaul witnessed the burgeoning of urbanism: removal of fortifications, growth of towns located at trading crossroads, stimulated by traffic that was facilitated by economic

23

progress and the development of better roads. Large roads leave Lyons and reach the most distant points of the territory: the Rhine, the Channel of Pas-de-Calais, the ocean, Aquitaine, Narbonnaise. It is necessary to contrast this with a map of modern transportation routes to understand the role that the choice of a capital can play in determining the transportation network. Note however, from this period, Lutetia (the site of Paris) became an important centre.

Thus patterned on a gridiron, dotted with towns endowed with classical monuments of Roman civilization, her youth drafted into the army, Gaul was transformed, and if townsmen multiplied, if towns were embellished, likewise the countrysides changed countenance: the monopolizing, in certain regions, of the best lands by the colonist, the clearing or improving of other lands elsewhere, made possible the creation of large estates, the construction of *villae* beside small holdings which subsisted in numbers; and in the Midi especially, the perpendicular geometry in the design of the land tracts is still related to the cadastral survey of this period. The toponymy (the endings of place names in ville, ac, etc.) as well as innumerable archaeological discoveries, and the majestic monuments reveal the magnitude of this influence which is responsible for the structure of the French landscapes at least in the Mediterranean Midi, the most fertile plains and plateaux of the east, the northeast, and the Paris basin, and is strongly marked in many other areas. It has sometimes been pointed out that the antiquity of the deforestation in Lorraine was attested to by the permanence of Gallo-Roman place-names. The stability of the communal limits, the precocity and coherence of village communities, the perfection of systems of crop rotation and of community customs were probably, for a large part, the fruits of an extensive romanization.

Finally, Rome brought to Gaul not only the organizing ability of the Latin genius, but she also furnished her with the germs and the vehicle of Christianity which, diffused from the fourth century on, was to profoundly mark French life in subsequent centuries and inscribe itself in the landscape by the majestic beauty of her cathedrals, by the establishment of her abbeys which often became generators of settlement or embryos of urban nuclei. The Catholic church, conceived from the outset as a visible gathering place and a tangible homage to the grandeur of God, became, then remained in the course of the centuries the heart of the village or small town, the central focus of urban quarters. Romanization and Christianization have largely contributed, despite the intervening time, to the shaping of present-day France.

The infiltrations of the 'barbarians' occurred gradually. As early as the second half of the third century, the Salian Franks settled as far as the Boulonnais (department of the Pas-de-Calais). Later they advanced as far as the Loire, while other Germanic peoples from beyond the Rhine valley came in waves toward the east and the centre. But the conditions were different in northern Gaul, rapidly occupied and transformed, from those in southern Gaul where up until the middle of the sixth century, the Aquitains were considered by the Franks as *Romani*. The disappearance of the *pax romana* was accompanied by profound modifications. Towns, menaced in their economic prosperity, sometimes despoiled by the waves of Germanic conquerors, retired behind high defensive walls often made of blocks torn away from the monuments of an earlier prosperous period. Nîmes, formerly a large flourishing city which occupied 220 hectares, only encircled 32 of them; Autun shrank from 200 hectares to 11 hectares. The changes were not as discernible in rural areas: a large part of the territory remained covered with forests and agriculture was confined rather to the well-drained plateaux, to the *ager* (cultivated lands), while vast areas of *saltus* (wooded lands) remained forested and were used often only for livestock. A certain number of *villae* (roman farm) were abandoned but many subsisted and to them were added nuclei of barbarous colonists who had been progressively implanted in the empire before its ruin, and later had accompanied the progress of the Germanic conquest. However, Roman Gaul was never very populated, nor very largely deforested. It was left to the centuries of the Middle Ages to give more or less to the French territory certain of its essential characteristics.

The shaping of the Middle Ages

It is not the purpose of this book to trace the evolution of the Middle Ages in detail, but rather to underscore the prominent facts.

Rural settlement occupies a conspicuous position. As early as the sixth century, Gregory of Tours mentions the bringing into cultivation of uncultivated lands, the creation of new farms, the planting of vineyards. Timid, disorganized and sometimes regressive in the periods of weak political power and limited demographic development, the occupation of the land made leaps and bounds when a stable political authority permitted it to, as under Charlemagne, who ordered his representatives to 'cut clearings in the forests' and the administrators of his royal domains to 'work the vineyards'; or, when the population pressure obliged men to tackle the natural environment in order to draw from it an increased sustenance. However, between the sixth and the eleventh century, progress was only sporadic and often temporary. Early in this period some areas were very populated, well utilized, and a kind of triennial crop rotation was applied — as around Paris — while other areas, in the west for example, were still largely occupied by a few large, scattered domains between which crept small properties of little consequence.

But from the eleventh century everything changed, and between 1050 and 1300, two vast movements of expansion of the cultivated lands began: deforestation and draining of marshes. This evolution was not particular to France, but general in Western Europe. People have pondered over the origin of this fundamental phenomenon: 'Fragmentation of rural exploitations, multiplication of new towns and small market-towns, development of cities, multiplication of parishes, proliferation of monasteries, crusades in Spain and in the Holy Land, everything postulates an increased number of men' (Joris, 1970). The same author reports that a sample survey in Picardy shows that the percentage of large families having from 8 to 12 or 15 children went from 9 per cent around 1120 to 42 per cent in 1210! Even if this is only a question of an exceptional and very localized occurrence, it translates

25

certainly a general tendency. This is confirmed by a fourteenth-century text from Briançon, declaring crudely: 'There are two-thirds too many people or at least a half' and Blanchard (1956), in his conclusion on the western Alps, wrote: 'The Alps in the middle of the medieval period were completely occupied and exploited.' The colonies settled in the valleys about the eleventh century, began from the twelfth to the six-teenth centuries, to intensively destroy the forests on the valley slopes, up to altitudes over 1000 metres, in order to put the soil under cultiva-tion. From this resulted a kind of disaster: the woods were destroyed by fire; the land was fertile for a few years and exhausted; it was then necessary to burn farther away, in order to regenerate the soils, and thus started, in certain cases, the erosion of the slopes, the disappear-ance of the thin layer of arable land, and the irreversible destruction of the forest cover. In the plains, the circumstances were not so unfavour-able: around the villages, the new lands gained by deforestation increased the arable area, while hamlets of colonization settled in the forests of the east and enlarged the fields at the expense of wooded areas.

This colonization developed especially in northern France which, after the thirteenth century, became by a kind of reversal from that which took place in the time of the Roman occupation and civilization, the most populated, the best exploited, and the richest region of the territory. During these same periods several marshy regions were drained; thus in Flanders, in Poitou where the first polders began to make their appearance. Everyone participated in this enterprise: the lords and their serfs, the landowners, small or large, the monasteries whose burgeoning, at the same period, was often accompanied by large areas of systematic colonization. Translating this agricultural prosperity, the mills for crushing the wheat, the production of oil, etc., multiplied. Eleven mills were constructed in Troyes between 1157 and 1191, five new ones in Rouen during the same century. In the domains of the Abbey of Cluny around 1150 – a generic model – 'the harvest reaches four to six times the seed committed to earth', but the normal yield was from two to two-and-a-half times the seed, and the results were not as good as this everywhere.

Parallel to this rural development, to this multiplication of villages, began a large urban movement. Production generated increased exchanges, and the fairs and markets flourished: 'In 1180, the fairs of Champagne and Brie succeeded one another throughout the year' (Joris, 1970). The lords, realizing the importance of these meetings for the prosperity of their possessions, granted towns numerous fair licenses. This permitted the development of commerce, cottage industry, the gathering of men, and thus were created new types of towns, which protected themselves with ramparts and obtained from their lords 'charters' of communal freedom. Consequently, at the end of the twelfth century, a new image of the city emerged from these transformations: a densely inhabited place with crowded houses, with majestic monuments and churches, elegant businesses, prosperous craftsmen and, in this expansion which characterized Amiens, Dijon, Rouen, Lille, Caen, Tours, Paris took a place of first importance.

Protected by stone ramparts which extended beyond both banks of the Seine, she was adorned with a Royal Palace, the first Louvre, built by Philippe-Auguste, outside the city wall around 1190; the choir of Notre-Dame was consecrated in 1182. She had the reputation of attracting those who were far away and appeared already as the 'royal city' *par excellence*.

However, this expansion of the Middle Ages was to know a long period of interruption with the ravages and disasters of the Hundred Years War (1338—1453). This war spread through most of the country situated between the Loire, the Seine and the Somme, while certain parts of France, as Languedoc or Brittany remaining outside the operations, maintained a relative prosperity. It was estimated that the French population diminished one-third during this period, which includes the ravages of the great plague of 1348—49.

The making of a modern nation

In this progressive development of the French territory, the importance of the European location must never be forgotten: involved closely in the history of neighbouring countries, France was in turn invaded or conquering. The mingling of peoples was permanent, the exchanges constant. Our territory was not a closed world; it was not protected by a girdle of seas; it was permeable. Its isthmus situation was permanently operative: the important routes were organized in terms of this position. The pilgrims of Saint-James of Compostella traversed the centre and the west and the pilgrimage churches marked this route; connections between the Venetian world and the Flemish world were made in part across the eastern part of the territory and the great fairs, the famous courts of the Dukes of Burgundy in Dijon, the Counts of Champagne in Troyes, bore witness to these routes. Trading with England developed and the ports were spread along the two coasts of the Channel; the east was attracted by the Rhine valley and the south by the Mediterranean basin. The interruption of the great trade flowing through this basin, disturbed by the Arab expansion was certainly strongly felt by the regions of southern France and, for a certain time, slowed down their progress. Thus the different parts of the territory developed, often in relation with the area beyond its frontiers as much as with the stimulation of the central government. The monetary economy penetrated the countrysides, and the towns grew, becoming centres of craftsmen and businessmen; in many cases dominated by a rich middle class which made a strong mark by the magnificence of its constructions both communal and private, by the organization of extremely profitable rural domains around urban areas. The lords and the nobility possessed the splendour, the military or official power, and more and more the middle class possessed the money, and especially the habit of earning it and making it profitable.

In the course of history, the French territory took on the political character by which we know it, and three equally important aspects of the formation of landscapes should be remembered. First of all, there exist a regional variety and a provincial life, reinforced by history: these are not only dependent on the fragmented diversity of the natural

27

conditions or on the originality of a particular population having its own civilization and sometimes its own language (as Brittany). They also are expressed little by little in the administrative and military system upon which, from the time of Charlemagne rested the defence of the empire, before turning into quasi-independent feudal fiefs. Still later they are expressed in the administrative circumscriptions of the kingdom. Certain provincial limits still explain some customs or differences in the landscape, and many are found again in the modern administrative boundaries of the planning regions created by the reform of 1955, after the fragmentation into departments established by the Revolution.

On the other hand in the beginning of the seventeenth century, unification was accomplished under the power of the French monarchy and the territory soon reached the Rhine, the Alps, the Pyrenees, that is to say the famous 'natural frontiers'. Finally the capital was fixed in the Paris region, after having wandered about tied to the rhythm of the journeys of kings and nobles who, for several centuries built and lived in the magnificent châteaux that burgeoned along the banks of the Loire: Blois, Amboise, Chambord, etc. But Louis XIV established Court at Versailles and Paris was confirmed in its position as capital. The successive ramparts, whose position is found in the outline of the boulevards which today cut the city into a series of crowns, illustrate Paris's vitality. She must have had about 400 000 inhabitants in the time of Louis XIV, and reached a half-million under the First Empire.

Parallel to this political maturation, the French territory continued its economic and demographic evolution. There were probably about 19 million inhabitants around 1680 and 28 million at the beginning of the nineteenth century. New methods and technical progress were circulating. France participated in the Agrarian Revolution: the suppression of fallow land, that came from the Netherlands and England, began on our territory in Flanders and spread progressively across the entire country. An agricultural economy and a rural population predominated and at the beginning of the nineteenth century, barely 7 per cent of the population was counted in cities of 20 000 inhabitants and more. Industries developed and the Industrial Revolution, which had first touched England, spread in France from the eighteenth century, but with a certain slowness and a certain moderation. The countryside resisted longer in France than in the countries of North-western Europe, because it was in the hands of a small peasantry, solidly rooted and very traditional; it was transformed only slowly. However, the cities took on more and more economic and spatial importance, and the landscapes changed.

The eighteenth century had marked the beginning of a new era with certain transformations of the countrysides. The era of the Physiocrats expressed itself in France by the attention large landowners paid to rural problems, the localized but spectacular amelioration, such as the transformation of the *Landes** of Gascony at the beginning of the

---

* Low-lying, sandy plains bordered by sand dunes, especially applied to the district of this name in southwest France.

nineteenth century. On the contrary the exploitation of coal developed slowly; before the appearance of the railroads, inadequate transportation, particularly by water, paralysed the growth of large industry, and urbanization progressed at a fairly moderate pace up until the second half of the nineteenth century. Industrialization did not engender, as in the neighbouring States, particularly Belgium, Germany, the United Kingdom, large industrial agglomerations except in the Nord and, after 1875, in northern Lorraine. This is perhaps also partially due to the relative demographic stagnation: between 1801 and 1940 the French population only increased by 50 per cent, passing from 28 million inhabitants to 42 million inhabitants, while at the same period that of the United Kingdom or the Netherlands almost quadrupled and that of Europe as a whole increased by 280 per cent. France was, in 1801, the most populous State on the continent; she was only in fifth place in 1940. Thus France did not know upheavals as spectacular and as massive as those which effected her neighbours in the course of the nineteenth and the beginning of the twentieth centuries. Large cities were not as numerous, nor as proliferating; industry was not as widespread and not as powerful; France remained much more rural and the transformation of the countrysides was more modest; while, encouraged by an abusive concentration of diverse means and by the centralization of political power, the capital knew a disproportionate development.

Today's originality

This renders the originality of the present period even more appreciable. It can be said that since the second half of the twentieth century, France has been making up for lost time, and for the observer who crosses this country, after having travelled through it 30 years ago, there is much to surprise him. The French landscapes are once again in the midst of evolution, the countrysides as well as the cities.

First of all, demographically, thanks to a family policy, set up in 1938 and reinforced constantly since then, the French population began to grow more rapidly. It went from 40.5 million inhabitants in 1946 to 52 million in 1974. This change of pace, this expansion of young people, demanding and voracious consumers from all points of view, imposes the construction of housing, the altering of numerous sectors of the economy, the upheaval of many traditions.

In the second place, the decrease in the agricultural working population is rapid; it went from 9.5 million persons, in 1946, to approximately 6 million at the present time, under the impetus of mechanization, modernization of production methods, but also due to the abandonment of the rural profession, judged to be too hard, too constraining and insufficiently remunerative. This produces as a consequence an important change in the physiognomy of the rural areas and is accompanied by a renewed proliferation of urbanization and a pressing need for the development of other activities, particularly industry. France is trying to fill in her undeniable gap in this domain.

Because of the necessity of these accelerated transformations, succeeding the post-war period, where reconstruction had demanded an enormous national effort, it appeared impossible to entrust to chance or to the good will of free enterprise the whole of these tasks. Thus a new policy has been adopted. Already planning, as far back as 1946, showed a desire for direction in putting order back into the territory shortly after the conflict. The creation in 1945 of a *Direction du Ministère de la Reconstruction* (Directorate of the Ministry of Reconstruction) had as its aim to 'regionalize' to some degree the decisions planned; by way of land problems this organization tried above all to act upon the administration of cities. The planned development of the territory is something other than the preparation and careful application of town plans, as Claudius Petit, one of the fathers of planned territorial development in France, affirmed in 1950. 'Planned development always considers the country in motion; it cannot start *tabula rasa* and remodel a continent, a region, a city, a landscape, without submitting to the constraints of the past. . . . But it does not live in the present; it must always be ahead of it, project on the future . . .' These are the reflections written after two years of responsibilities by Olivier Guichard, the first Delegate to the national organization for planned development and regional action (*Délégué à l'Aménagement du Territoire et à l'Action Régionale*), when it was created in France on 14 February 1963. And he continued: 'The planned development of the territory makes us proceed from a spontaneous, immediate and economic occupation (subsistence development) to the voluntary organization of a city, a region, or an entire territory.'

The development was progressive. The preoccupations of regional development, at once integrated into the Plan, were transcribed in 1955, in the form of 'regional plans', corresponding to a subdivision of the French territory into 21 planning regions (see p. 100). These regions are highly dissimilar in size and population. The smallest, Alsace, includes only two departments, but groups nevertheless about 1 400 000 inhabitants; the largest regions, Midi-Pyrenees (eight Departments) or Rhône–Alps (also eight Departments), are heterogeneous groupings, uniting portions of high mountains (Pyrenees or Alps), plains (those of the Aquitaine Basin or the valleys of the Saône and Rhône), and portions of ancient massifs (edges of the Central Massif). The most populous is, of course, the Paris region, with nearly 10 million inhabitants, while the least densely populated are the Limousin (750 000 inhabitants) and Franche-Comté (970 000). Another heterogeneity lies in the dominating power of the principal urban centre: if several of these regions depend upon the action generated by one important city, as the Paris region with Paris, Nord with Lille, Alsace with Strasbourg, Rhône–Alps with Lyons, Provence–Côte d'Azur with Marseilles, Aquitaine with Bordeaux, Midi-Pyrenees with Toulouse, in other regions, the largest city is often only of modest dimensions, capable of providing by itself a moderate economic stimulus. However, what is homogeneous, is the administrative structure placed under the direction of a Regional Prefect, who is appointed by the Government. Thus a new structure was created whose efficacy, in many domains, can already be measured.

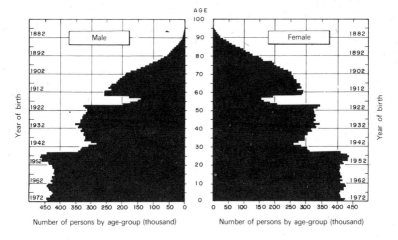

Fig. 4   Population of France
          Evaluation at 1 January 1973

Finally it is necessary to take into consideration a final distinctive fact: France is a country which is not populated on the European scale. She counts 92 inhabitants per square kilometre, against 226 in the United Kingdom, 241 in West Germany, 375 in the Netherlands and 174 in Italy, whose territory is much more broken. The intensity of human occupation is then inevitably less. In France numerous natural landscapes remain almost empty of people, and at this time, many vast regional or national parks are being created, reserves of green areas for the crowded Europeans. This paucity of human cover is felt in the development of certain land areas as well. If our best lands are well cultivated, many relatively poorer lands are abandoned; in the mountains, many areas formerly cultivated return to fallow lands. When one passes from France into Belgium, by the routes of Ardenne, or from France into Switzerland, in the Geneva area, one can measure the difference. Pressed by necessity neighbouring countries carefully clear and cultivate fields which in France would be abandoned and neglected.

Part Two

The Rural Landscapes

Introduction

France is a country with strong rural traditions, where for a long time farming has been one of the major sources of economic wealth. The old adage of Sully 'Tilling and grazing are the lifeblood of France' bears witness to this for the past, while the statistics of the working population at the beginning of the twentieth century show that, even quite recently, agriculture exercised an important role in France. Around 1920 it still occupied 37.5 per cent of the working population, while in the United Kingdom this proportion was reduced to 7 per cent.

Shaped by this long and powerful domination, the countryside presents complex aspects, where the most contrasting characteristics are found either assembled in a coherent whole, or mingled in inextricable combinations. The inertia of certain traits, such as the boundaries, the layout of roads, the shape of the land plots, the location and arrangement of dwellings, has been fostered by the traditionalism of rural societies for long poorly equipped technically, by the solidity of stone constructions, defying time and even the ravages of war, by the long continuance of the same products necessary for daily life. However, changes have infiltrated or have been imposed under the influence of certain key factors — either internal: demographic pressure or regression, transformation of social classes and evolution of attitudes and of agrarian techniques — or external: the rise of modern means of communication, the development of agricultural speculation, the improvement of methods and material.

3
Evolution and principal elements

The three main stages of evolution

The French rural landscapes were created in the course of an evolution which lasted several millenia. Schematically, three fundamental stages are distinguished.

The conquest of the soil and the working of the land continued for centuries with one essential preoccupation: subsistence. Unlike their successors, the men who participated in it were not concerned with adapting the rural modes of life to the particular characteristics of each type of soil; instead, they preferred to repeat indefinitely the application of a single type of development over vast areas, going beyond the framework of the natural regions. Cereals predominated nearly everywhere, associated with a few additional crops necessitated by the most elementary daily needs (garden vegetables, fruit trees, textiles like flax or hemp, certain forage, etc.). They even persisted in producing wine, indispensable to Catholic worship, as far as northern France. From the thirteenth century, a few communes, well situated near important trading routes, were exclusively dedicated to viticulture (near Collioure, Auxerre), but it was not until the seventeenth century that the vine disappeared from Flanders and Normandy, or until the nineteenth that it deserted the hills in the centre of the Paris basin. Agriculture was based upon the association of tillage—pasture; the problem of their coexistence dominated all rural structures and all the modalities of their incorporation into the landscape.

The second stage began with the development of transportation. The opening of roads where carriages moved incessantly, and especially the cutting of canals, then the advent of railroads, revolutionized production in rural areas. Exchange permitted both specialization and speculation. In terms of its own particular aptitudes, each region was able to choose the crops for which it was the most naturally suited. Consequently, we see the disappearance of this uniformity of production which had struck Arthur Young (at the end of the eighteenth century), for example, across the whole 'vast and fertile plain that almost without interruption, stretches from Flanders almost to Orléans'. On the contrary, in the nineteenth century, 'regions' become distinct. André Thibault (1967, 17—32) minutely studying the agricultural evolution of the Picardy plateau wrote:

In 1850, today's agricultural regions did not yet exist; from the land,

35

light or heavy, moist or dry, people asked a living. . . . The natural heterogeneity of the Picardy plain, to which the Bray can be added, is effaced by a human milieu that is identical in its main lines. Certainly, there is a beginning of the division into natural regions, but not into original human environments. Furthermore none of these natural environments has an imperious vocation for cereals, sugar-beets, or grazing. This will become evident only when modern civilization has upset the former balance by its means of transportation, its alimentary needs, its notions of profit. In the face of all these factors, human societies, relying on the possibilities of the natural environments, have reacted differently.

The third stage characterizes contemporary agricultural development. Technological power has become such that speculation alone regulates the land use. Market gardening, indispensable to the supplying of large cities and pushed back by the development of suburbs, invades the former wheat lands with vegetables cultivated in the openfields, as around Paris and the eastern part of the Beauce; covers vast areas of alluvial terraces as in the *varennes* (local name for alluvial plains around Tours) in the Loire valley or on the outskirts of Toulouse; takes over the irrigated lands of the lower-Rhône plains. According to the fluctuations of official prices and of legislation, the sugar-beet increases or curtails its domination of the northern plains and of the central part of the Paris basin; we tear out the vineyards of Languedoc, the apple trees planted in the meadows of Normandy, but we replant the vine-stocks in Burgundy and in the Loire valley and the apple orchards generally. To spontaneous evolution is often added a guided transformation.

The succession of these three stages is perfectly illustrated in the vicissitudes of 'Dry' or 'Dusty' Champagne and of Languedoc. In Languedoc by nature 'excessive and rough', historical texts show that, up until the beginning of the eighteenth century, cereals, animal husbandry, vegetable farming, contend with the vine, whose profits became established around the end of the seventeenth century, as a subsistence economy gave way to a market economy. 'The growth of the wine industry is the offspring of commerce rather than climate even if the latter prompts olive-tree growers, disgusted by the successive frosts, or the sowers of cereals, dreading the drought and the shrivelling of crops in the summer, to turn to the vine. The areal expansion is based upon a qualitative progress which commands the marketing possibilities' (Dermigny, 1967). From this moment on, the rise of viticulture, reinforced by the consequences of the phylloxera blight in 1875, was not to stop and eventually made the entire coastal plain, between the Rhône delta and the foothills of the eastern Pyrenees, a vast region of monoculture. This situation lasted until just after the Second World War. At that point, the marketing difficulties of this wine — inconsistent in quality and often mediocre — on a nation-wide saturated market, led to a voluntary policy of partial destruction of the vineyards and, thanks to the development of irrigation through a canal fed by the Rhône waters, the introduction of new crops (Dermigny and Brunet, 1967).

As for Dry Champagne, Roger Dion showed that this region, for centuries good cereal land, acquired its reputation for poverty when grazing was developed, necessitating rich grasslands, and the unfertile chalklands proved incapable of sustaining them. For two centuries, Champagne thus became a rejected region, until around 1935—40 when a few large landowners made the necessary investments, ploughed deeply, added considerable quantities of fertilizer to enrich the poor soil, and succeeded in producing not only good harvests, but even crops of beets on the bare chalk, which seemed absolutely inconceivable a few decades earlier (Dion, 1961, 209—19).

Thus each French region would necessitate a detailed description in order to analyse how the present landscape is the resultant of multiple interactions. This method would be too long and tedious. However, throughout the countryside, certain features recur, groups of characteristics are found together, and it is possible to suggest common explanations illustrated by specific examples.

What then are *the essential characteristics of a rural landscape*? To begin with, we notice what is deeply engrained and cannot be changed quickly. The first thing that strikes our attention is the look of the land: are the land plots open or enclosed, large or small, regular in form or not? Are characteristic orientations discernible? The study of the settlement is closely related to that of the land; the observer, in a single glance, takes them both in, whether he is in the field or looking at a map or an aerial photograph. Next, we notice the land use, certain aspects of which are quasipermanent, as the distribution of the forests, while other aspects are fluctuating, as the type of crops.

Classic rural landscapes

Two names — Lorraine and western Normandy — suffice to mark the extreme contrasts which exist in French rural landscapes.

Openfield

Lorraine is, *par excellence*, the classic openfield province. The land is made up of an imbrication of open fields, generally oblong, often slightly curved; as the name indicates, no boundary separates one from another, and only the orientation of the furrows and the type of crop enable one to distinguish one field from the other. A part of the land, sometimes peripheral and coincident with an accident in the relief (summit of a *cuesta*, edge of a plateau, butte) is still occupied by the forest. The village is rigorously grouped, generally the houses with severe and monotonous façades are contiguous and aligned along streets intersecting at right angles; frequently, at the major intersection of these streets, is the village square with its church, town hall, school, and a few shops. Behind the deep houses, occupying a long and narrow piece of land perpendicular to the streets lie a courtyard, farm buildings, and often a vegetable garden. Outside the village, whence radiate roads and paths, dividing the land into several triangles, are found practically no isolated dwellings, except for a few rare and vast farms, or some modern dwelling. There are no trees in the fields; when a valley crosses the land, it is like a band of greenery, accompanied by meadows enclosed with hedges.

This type of pure openfield is found in the northern and western parts of the Paris basin. In the Tertiary plateaux between the Seine and the Oise, it has been described as a 'mosaic openfield' with the same general characteristics as the Lorraine model (Brunet, 1960, 545). However, the form and the size of the fields are clearly different: these average about 10 hectares, and frequently go up to 50 or 60 hectares. Though very large, they remain predominantly oblong. The simple contours of the square or the rectangle give way to trapezoidal forms, related to the radiating network of old paths that subsist and between which they are inscribed. These large fields occupy all the land in the commune, with the exception of the gardens that are adjacent to the houses of the villages and into which they merge without transition. The settlement is agglomerated, but it is only in the western part of the Multien that it is perfectly grouped. In the region of Ile-de-France and most of the Valois, a few rare isolated farms are interspersed between the villages; in the eastern part of the Multien, the northern part of the Valois, and the Soissonnais, the farms are more numerous; sometimes even, as in the Coulommiers region, near the Marne valley, only a scattering of farms occur.

This same type of landscape extends also into the north-eastern part of Burgundy (Senonais, Châtillonnais), in the northern Saône plains, where grouped settlement and openfields in clusters of narrow strips prevail. Beyond the Seine valley, the Beauce is a magnificent example of a mosaic-openfield with grouped villages and occasionally interspersed farms.

But in the Paris basin itself appear gradations of this type of landscape: in the *Pays de Caux* are found numerous enclosed pastures around inhabited areas and houses at wide intervals, permitting the villages to stretch out along the roads for long distances (2 to 7 km for certain villages in the *Pays de Caux*). In Berry or in Touraine, or around Caen, the *champagnes*, even if they are not as bare as in Beauce, are relatively open and despite some patches of wood contrast with the neighbouring *bocages*, by the appearance of their land as much as by their settlement, which tends to agglomerate in large hamlets or even villages. Thus we pass through a kind of transitional area between the regions with predominantly openfields in the northeast and those with enclosed fields, which are prevalent most everywhere else except Provence (Juillard *et al.*, 1957, 165).

However, more or less extensive islands of openfield, of *champagne* (a term which does not mean as is too often thought 'presence of limestone', but 'conditions favouring the formation of a group of small-scale cultivators' (Dion, 1934, 163)) are found to some extent in all French regions. They have been described in the southern part of Limagne (Derruau, 1949, 545), in the plateaux of the Jura in the north-eastern part of Upper-Bugey (Lebeau, 1955, 604), in Périgord, in the Rhône valley, in the Ariège valley of the central Pyrenees, and even in Brittany, in the Pont—Château region, in the Rhuis peninsula (Meynier in Juillard *et al.*, 1957). Certain valleys of the Béarn region, others in

Charente and in the centre of the Aquitaine basin also offer localized examples. These isolated *champagnes* differ from the large open regions of the northeast: they are not so bare, their settlement is less agglomerated, their village designs are more rounded, they are closely spaced and frequently accompanied by a string of dispersed dwellings.

Bocage

In western Normandy as well as in parts of Maine, Anjou, Vendée, Poitou, the *bocage* prevails. It can be contrasted feature by feature with the openfield landscape.

The land of the commune is made up of plots enclosed by hedges planted on high mounds of earth dominating a ditch; these enclosures are irregular in shape, but without much difference between the two dimensions. The entire countryside is fragmented: grass and trees occupy a predominant place; small woods and forest remnants subsist in numbers; traffic moves along sunken lanes bordered by thick and bushy hedgerows. The settlement is dispersed: the main nucleus which groups services is surrounded by numerous hamlets formed by three or four farms or even, in numerous cases, the farms are isolated from one another; the farms are composed of scattered buildings, arranged within a green enclosure. From afar or from a bird's-eye view, one can scarcely distinguish the houses which are hidden amid the greenery.

This landscape fragmented by hedgerows is widespread throughout western France, but it also penetrates the openfield regions, for example in the Boulonnais and the Hainaut; this landscape is likewise found in south-western Burgundy (Gâtinais, Puisaye, Morvan and its fringes), in south-western Bugey, the region of Gex, Savoy, the northern part of the Central Massif, the south-western part of the Basque region and certain parts of the centre of the Aquitaine basin.

In numerous regions where broken stone is abundant, the hedgerow is replaced by the dry wall, more or less bonded, when the material lends itself (Jurassic limestone in regular flat pieces), or loose, combining the functions of boundaries and of piling up cleared stones, as in Brittany, in the centre of the Central Massif, etc.

Mediterranean landscape

Another type of landscape is found in the Midi, including the south-eastern edge of the Central Massif as well as the eastern Pyrenees and the southern Alps, but particularly characteristic in Provence: it is the *Mediterranean landscape*, which merits separate mention.

Here the fields are very rarely enclosed; the limits are indicated by markers, a solid and old tradition still used in the middle of the nineteenth century; the markers consist of a large stone accompanied by two smaller ones, fixed at the corner of the plots. The horizon is open from one hill to the next, and while travelling no obstacles are met other than the canals in irrigated zones and the rows of cypress trees or reeds which regularly divide the cultivated areas of the Comtat plains and of the irrigated Crau plains; these rows have no connection with the land division, but are planted solely in relation to the direction of the *mistral*, a harmful wind whose force they break by presenting repeated obstacles, perpendicular to its path. Stone walls are found only around cities or small market-towns where they limit town property, or else in steps along slopes where they support terraces. These terraces, narrow horizontal strips of land which follow the contour-lines and transform the hillsides into tiers are a major feature of the Mediterranean landscape. The form of the fields is distinctly square, whether the plots are small or large; oblong plots are not completely absent, but much less developed than in the north (Livet, 1962). Settlement is mixed: grouped villages, very often perched on hilltops and numerous, varied dispersed settlements including even the isolated *mas* (small farmhouse in the south of France) which dot the plains (Livet, 1962, 465).

Checker-Board landscape

Lastly, scattered across the territory, occupying generally the low-lying perfectly horizontal plains, is also found a very strict checker-board landscape, emphasized by a gridiron pattern of canals (as in maritime Flanders, in the marshlands of Dol and of Vendée) or by a gridiron type road pattern (lower Durance, Comtat, etc.). This purely geometrical and regular layout contrasts with the complex and often heterogeneous forms that are generally found in the French territory as a whole.

Openfields and enclosed fields

Openfield and *bocage*, these are the two most dissimilar landscapes that can be found. On the basis of their general localization — regionally very different — people have tried to relate the *bocage* either to natural conditions (a more humid west) or to the survival of former ethnic traditions (the individualism attributed to the Celts in the west) and the 'openfield' to the community spirit evidenced by populations from the eastern part of France penetrated by germanic influences or more romanized. These theories have been discussed and disputed; scholars now tend to veer more willingly toward the influence of economic and social conditions during the last centuries of the Middle Ages and modern times.

The enclosure appears to be the result of the struggle between tillers and stock-breeders, or rather between cultivation and grazing. On the landscape it represented efforts made to protect certain plots from the free wandering or repeated passage of a herd. This seems to be the conclusion generally accepted by the most competent French authors, historians or geographers, who have tackled this problem, either in a general way, or by examining particular local or regional examples in the course of recent decades. Marc Bloch (1951, 266), Roger Dion (1934; 1946, 6—80), Etienne .Juillard and André Meynier (Juillard *et al.*, 1957) are among the most illustrious writers who have given credence to this point of view*.

It appears that the various peoples who little by little developed the French territory depended on milk, cheese, meat, as well as on cereals

* This section is a restatement of the ideas expressed by these authors.

and a few other crops for their subsistence. This was perhaps already the result of an adaptation from a pastoral to a sedentary way of life. The preoccupation of feeding the herd was therefore fundamental. At the same time, it was necessary to protect the cultivated plots from the appetites of the livestock and, from the beginning of the Middle Ages, temporary fences were built or a ditch dug around each group of fields. After harvest-time, these temporary obstacles were removed. This custom was discontinued in the twelfth and thirteenth centuries, when a closer and stricter organization of the lands rendered it useless and on the contrary led to the building of durable enclosures between the tilled area and the pastureland. Thus, very early, the Lorraine village itself was encircled by a more or less large ring of 'enclosures', where the peasant was master of his land; beyond that began the *ban*, the collective open area, bound by communal rules.

From the end of the Middle Ages, social evolution moved toward a fragmentation of the *ban* — the only possibility for agrarian progress. During the fifteenth and sixteenth centuries, the middle class, by way of quitrent payment, had lands ceded to them that they were allowed to enclose, and where they set up farms at the edge of communal lands. Numerous regions showed a very definite tendency toward the complete appropriation of plots, including the freedom to utilize them as desired. In the eighteenth century, enlightened agriculturists denounced the right of common as one of the most harmful practices. Even though the edicts of enclosure which, at the instigation of the Physiocrats, were promulgated from 1767 on, were too generous to be really effective, they nevertheless had significant local results. In Béarn, for example, it was stipulated in 1767 that all inherited property should be enclosed, including the lands formerly reserved for common grazing. But above all, these edicts articulated an attitude which had long been manifest throughout the French countrysides, and which had diverse results, depending upon the conditions of the natural environment and the mentalities of the populations concerned.

In north-eastern France, three factors seem to have coincided: the existence of vast calcareous plateaux, sufficiently drained and generally covered with *limon*; the presence of relatively dense populations, occupying areas which had been developed long before, as is evidenced by the remains of the *Campignienne* civilization among others, and the strong traces of the agrarian occupation during the Gallo-Roman period (Nougier, 1950) and especially the importance of groups with strong communal structures. The relative dryness prevailing in these areas made them unsuitable for grass, and in order to subsist, the herd had to depend on the stubble left after the harvest and on the fallow lands, which occupied the land one out of every three years according to the system of triennial crop rotation then practised. This was the system of fallow pastureland, used in common by all the village herds. Such a custom, which necessitated a strong collective discipline, entailed a whole set of strictly communal practices: the absence of boundaries between the plots, so as not to hinder the passage of the animals, the distribution of the lands among the inhabitants in such a way that all the fields in a certain area might be either cultivated or left fallow the same year, thus the acceptance by all of a particular rotation of crops, a cycle which generally operated over a period of three years in northern France and over two years in the south. Therefore, all of the tilled land was divided into three sections and all the lands in each section were used in the same way, the same year. Despite its drawbacks, notably the paralysis of all initiative and the impossibility of individual progress, this system lasted a very long time almost intact in the whole eastern part of the Paris basin, where the high density of occupation, and the difficulty of finding good grasslands outside the valleys due to geologic and climatic conditions, played a major role. On the other hand, to the west of a line joining Paris and the western part of Ardenne, everywhere where the moisture was sufficient and where the type of soil was suitable, the customary practice of leaving the land fallow was abandoned from the seventeenth century on and specialized fields came into being, especially from the eighteenth century, and were enclosed and often planted with trees, completely transforming the former open-field, as in Thiérache, in the *Pays de Caux*, in the Boulonnais. The communal practices were abandoned and, according to Roger Dion, 'grass was the emancipator' of the western regions of the Paris basin.

In western France, where the climate was more humid and the terrain was often impermeable and of inconsistent fertility, the natural conditions offered very different possibilities to the groups who undoubtedly settled in fewer numbers. Vast fallow lands extended around the ploughed land and served as common pasture. On the contrary, cultivated areas were enclosed, and farmers were masters of their own crop rotation; sometimes for reasons of economy, fences would enclose a group of land plots. As for the good grasslands, they soon became individual properties: originally, only the first cutting of hay was reserved for the owners of the land; then, all the village herds had access to any fresh growth. This system was very harmful to the quality of the grassland and wronged the owner as well. As there was no lack of pasture lands, people very rapidly began to also enclose the good meadows.

Thus agrarian individualism developed much more rapidly, resulting in a fragmented landscape, where the plots were protected, sometimes the meadows as in the Limousin, sometimes the fields, and sometimes both as in Brittany.

Nevertheless, in the very heart of these regions dominated by enclosures, subsist islands of open *champagne*, made up of clusters of small strips of fields, bounded externally by a fence. A detailed study of them has shown that they were the site of collective practices, of a real communal mutual aid (compulsory crop rotation in Brittany; grouping to perform agricultural work in the Midi). Their origin is not clear: some people attempted to explain it by the division of a former farm estate among too many heirs; others saw a Roman *villa* or a medieval *allodium* (freehold estate) divided among a group of humble people forming a kind of rural community. According to old maps, these areas were often larger and have been nibbled away by successive enclosures, leaving only the nucleus of the smallest plots that were almost impossible to enclose because of the high costs and the obstacles that would have been presented to cultivation. These *champagnes* are therefore the residue of an area occupied by very poor, humble people, having practised and sometimes still practising nowadays a certain type of collective economy: these are the conclusions of Roger Dion, taken up again by Etienne Juillard (Juillard *et al.*, 1957).

As for the Mediterranean landscape, it is the result of the settlement by extremely individualistic peoples. Research into the documents shows the scarcity of true fallow pasture and the peasants' marked tendency for agrarian autonomy that dates back a long time (Roger Livet, 1962). The farmer is master of his land, he chooses his crops and is free to decide his own rhythm of crop rotation which, here generally biennial, is not a rigorous obligation but is a flexible empirical method which makes it possible to palliate the deficiency of the soils that are dry and often deprived of farmyard manure; all this is accomplished without even being necessary to have recourse to a fence. The same is true for grazing: under certain conditions, it is permitted in the *garrigues* (area of low, sparse vegetation), in the forests on the hills, but is prohibited on cultivated lands, even unfenced under penalty of severe fines or even confiscation of the herd. All that is needed to indicate the prohibited area is a few rocks assembled in a certain way in the corner of the field. Thus, an open landscape and complete individualism coexist in all of south-eastern France.

Field patterns

Another very obvious characteristic of the agrarian landscape, although at first sight less important, is the shape of the fields. Nowhere does it seem to have been left to chance for, when seen from the air, the division into parcels of land in the various French regions is extremely varied. Essentially, two main types are distinguished: oblong fields and square fields. Certain authors such as Marc Bloch have systematically contrasted the long plots of the north with the more compact shapes of the south. The generalization is not quite so simple.

In Lorraine are still found long and narrow fields, slightly curved. Formerly, they must have prevailed in all the openfield regions. They are still very common in the *champagnes* disseminated across the entire territory. This shape seems to reflect social and economic influences and also technology. It is always the result of a subsequent division of a larger unit which might have been a former large estate, an area collectively cleared, communal holdings, etc. The division in the direction of the furrows was the easiest way to equalize the parts, and the parcelling enabled each one, heir or buyer, to obtain by a skilful sampling of the parcels, lands of all the different qualities. Moreover this oblong shape was related to the use, in the northern regions, of the plough, which required a fairly large space for turning; this led to the lengthening of the furrows in order to reduce the number of turns. The curving has been explained either as an adaptation to the undulation of the terrain, or by the deviation in the outline caused by the plough itself and accentuated by subsequent tillage.

These oblong parcels represented a stage in the division of the land.

They are still visible in aerial photographs particularly in many regions of the Paris basin, or else they have disappeared, brought together into the large fields of the mosaic-openfield, as a result of numerous success-ful efforts to regroup the lands. The first efforts were spontaneous. In the Soissonnais, around 1718, there was already a movement to concen-trate farms; the changes increase in the eighteenth and at the beginning of the nineteenth centuries; since the middle of the nineteenth century the number of large farms has changed very little. This concentration aimed at the cultivation of the land, not the ownership; it was brought about by exchanges or by the purchase of lands, and as a result, a farm of 250 to 350 hectares was now made up of no more than 15 to 20 parcels, assuring an adequate variety of soil types (Brunet, 1960). The fields are thus large, compact, easy to work, occupying all the area from one lane to the next. It is principally the plateaux which present this physiognomy, the valleys having remained much more fragmented.

At the present time an official redistribution of the land holdings is in progress. It is aimed at the entire French territory. It had been rendered indispensable by the excessive fragmenting which, already intensive before the Revolution, was accentuated by the legislation put into effect by the Civil Code under the First Empire, to such a degree that, around 1820, Benjamin Constant wrote: 'The division of property is the basis of the new French organization.' In 1891, there were 151 million plots of land in a cultivated area of 52 million hectares, that is an average of 35 acres or 0.9 of an acre per plot. Still, in 1946, the agricultural census showed an average of 42 plots per farm. The small size of each piece of land and their distance apart imposed heavy expenses: the cost price of the cultivation of 1 hectare of wheat went from 1 to 1.79 if the hectare was fragmented into six fields 300 metres apart. To this must be added the lost time and the difficulties of mechanization. Consequently, following the spontaneous impulse already mentioned, the legislature rendered the redistribution of lands official in 1918, but the results were slow, up until the new stimulus given after 1941—45, and over these last 25 years, the redistribution of lands has involved more than 6 million hectares, while the procedure is at presently in progress on nearly 12.5 million hectares, that is to say on more than one-third of France's agricultural lands. The entire Paris basin, broadly speaking, from Normandy to Lorraine and from Artois to the edge of the Central Massif and in Burgundy, is practically finished; the west-central region and the middle valley of the Rhône, are going well. These operations have provoked a considerable change in the rural landscape: tiny fields, stretched out in parallel strips or arranged in irregular checker-board patterns, have been replaced by large continuous areas of massive, but often irregular shapes. From the air one can often still distinguish the former pattern which is visible in the lighter ridges on the open land. The mosaic openfield is, in large part, the result of the combined efforts of the different periods of land redistribution, spontaneous then official (*La Doc. Française Ill.*).

In a certain number of regions, notably in the Mediterranean-Midi, the square shape of the fields has been stressed for a long time. The shaping correspond to a very old tradition. The influence of the *araire* (light plough) which is more easily manoeuvred than the *charrue* (heavy plough) and the custom of cross-ploughing, still practised in Provence, have been cited, but these are only technical reasons. The real origin of this square-type division has been ascribed by several authors to the colonization during the Roman period; these conquerors' predilection for perpendicular geometries, for simple and regular forms, is well known; various documents, in particular cartularies of the tenth and eleventh centuries already show these square forms which may go back to the Roman cadastral survey. This division would first have been drawn with precision around the inhabited or colonized areas, where the small square parcels multiplied. In the intervening areas, lands with the same shape increased, whether they were in the centre of large well-cultivated estates in the plains, or shared the poor lands of the *garrigue* and the forest, always according to the same principle. Thus, there are two very different types of land use: should we see in them two successive waves of settlement? The question remains unanswered.

In any case, the extreme partitioning of the land which characterizes the entire French territory was essentially in response to a concern to equalize everyone's chances at the time when either originally or progressively autonomous exploitations were established. In certain cases, this preoccupation produced some rather spectacular results, as for example the very special type of circular field patterns, which are found in the Montady pond, according to tradition drained already in the Roman period, but more probably by the monks in the thirteenth century, thanks to a network of radial canals, from the periphery toward the centre where a perfect circle accumulates the waters collected; a similar arrangement is found in only one other pond, much smaller, in the region of Pouzolle (Aude) (Soyer, 1965, 170).

The characteristics of modern exploitation and, particularly, the appearance of truck farming in the Comtat plain during the nineteenth century, advanced the division into small square fields; but the arrangement of the parcels is masked by the lines of cypress trees, which fragment the landscape into short strips whose parallel pattern extends for tens of kilometres. These cypress trees, planted 50 centimetres apart, form real barriers, which break the violent gusts of the *mistral*, blowing perpendicularly to them. Their spread dates back to the Second Empire, concurrently with the progress of truck farming; almost everywhere they replaced the hedges which existed previously in the Comtat plain. These rows of cypress trees have no value as fences, but cut the fields into sections.

The same is true, in a more general way, on all the mountain slopes in the southeast, fragmented into steps by the strips of terraces whose origins are difficult to state precisely. It is almost certain that some already existed in the Gallo-Roman period, and they are fairly widespread in all the neighbouring mountainous Mediterranean districts. Their chief purpose is to hold the soil on the slopes. Developed as a consequence of the combined effects of the relief, the climate and the concern for preserving the soils, they also served to better distribute the irrigation waters, when necessary. They experienced marked periods of expansion in the Middle Ages at the time of the rapid demographic

Fig. 5 Administrative unit where the lands have been regrouped: Oissery (Seine and Marne): former stage

increases during the twelfth and thirteenth centuries and of reconstruction in the fifteenth century, and also in the second half of the eighteenth century. We might wonder how such constructions were sucessfully completed: it seems that they were purely the result of individual efforts, although the division of the slopes that they represented could not have been carried out unless there was single ownership or agreement among different landowners. Today the terraces are largely abandoned owing to the numerous consequences of the rural exodus. They only subsist where highly profitable crops benefit from their precious micro-climate and use a soil that is often rare. They are still used by the well-known vineyards (as those of the Hermitage in the Rhône valley), those of the hills of Provence or of Roussillon, the

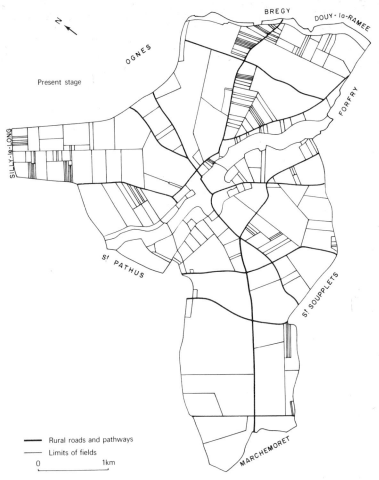

Fig. 6 Administrative unit where the lands have been regrouped: Oissery (Seine and Marne): present stage

orchards on the slopes of the middle valleys of Provence (for example the Gaperon), the floriculture in the hinterland of Menton, the greenhouses and truck farms which have recently multiplied west of Nice.

The technique of using the slopes, while fighting against soil erosion, the technique of draining the low, marshy plains or the coastal marshlands: in all these cases, the methods of gaining the land have imposed a rather geometric landscape (Wagret, 1959, 316). The polders stand out by a regular grid pattern, corresponding to the layout of the canals necessary for carrying off surplus water. The reclaiming of swamps is almost always the work of a powerful, stable, well-organized community, because the technical effort required must have been often

47

considerable and persistent. As in the case of the Flemish marshlands, foreign specialists were called in — in this case Dutch. After a recent invasion of the sea which occurred in the fifth century, the maritime Flemish plain was reclaimed between a row of dunes and the slight slope of the interior plain; the work lasted several centuries, and was the object of a systematic organization like the Dutch polders (a system of canals maintained by syndicates of landowners, the *wateringues*). In western France there was no systematic organization of the drainage except in the marshlands of Bas—Poitou; the improvement was especially the work of monks; undertaken before the eighth century by the abbots of Noirmoutiers, it was systematically continued from the tenth century onwards, but its actual form results from the action of Henry IV. Several royal edicts and the systematic action of Bradley and a certain number of his compatriots, accomplished the drainage of most of the marshlands from Normandy to Languedoc, with Aunis, Saintonge, Vendée, etc., in between. In the eighteenth century, stimulated by the ideas of the Physiocrats, a few prosperous landowners became interested in diking the lowlands, along the sea, in order to enlarge their property (islands of Ré, Oléron, Noirmoutiers, the littoral of Bourgneuf). In the Mediterranean-Midi, a few restricted draining operations were begun in the Middle Ages, near already existing villages (marshlands of Molliges in the thirteenth century, plain of Aubagne in the fifteenth century). The conquest of more extensive areas was more difficult: these works undertaken in the twelfth century in the marshlands of Arles lasted until the seventeenth century; the diking of the Lower-Durance at which the nobles, the riverside communities, and the monastic orders, worked unceasingly, was not completed until the nineteenth century. And still today, new lands have been reclaimed in the Camargue, in the Crau, near Tombolo d'Hyères.

Thus, by a meticulous effort, man has little by little divided and developed the French soil. The detailed study of the lands of one region in transitional areas like Périgord (Paul Fénelon) or Burgundy (Louis Champier) shows a juxtaposition of patterns which can well illustrate both the different modalities of land use around a nucleus of settlement and the successive stages of progress in the spatial conquest spreading out from an inhabited centre. Thus 'gardens' form around the houses a first zone of *meix* (or *cours* or *courtils*); then the *champagnes*, with their narrow strips almost always parallel, indicate the good lands early developed, while the 'plains' occupied by longer, unequal plots more or less regularly arranged, correspond to the lands of medium fertility, further from the centres and developed at a later date. To this can be added, in areas covered by forests, the geometric boundary of the cultivated areas conquered by slashing and burning (*essartage*) (Champier, 1956, 157—63).

Rural roads

All organization of rural landscapes begins by the laying out of roads which are a function of the tasks to be performed. The rural road is, according to Gaston Roupnel (1932, 431) 'the builder of the countryside and the distributor of the established order'. It is by the road or path that workers reach their place of work: the fields stem from it, are perpendicular to it, a feature that is still visible on large-scale maps of all the French regions. The road pattern radiating from the village, dividing the land into several triangular parcels (*soles*) is characteristic of the openfield landscapes in all northern and eastern France. On the other hand, each geologic subdivision comprises its own special group of plots, whose boundaries are frequently marked out by the paths or roads. The faults, which bring into contact different soils with diverse possible uses, are almost always followed by the earliest roads. In the Mediterranean-Midi, particularly in Provence, besides a great preponderance of patterns with radiating structures that are found in the steep hills as well as in the coastal plains and which appear extremely old, one meets also a checker-board network which always has as its origin an act of voluntary colonization, of a certain land in blocks. In a few cases, like the basins of the depressions in the Var, which have been occupied for a very long time, we may recall the Roman cadastral survey: the occupying forces expropriated the vanquished in order to redistribute their lands to the new holders, as was their custom. In other cases, those of the low-lying plains recently colonized, as the lands of the Lower-Durance and the Comtat, it is after drainage and definitive reclamation that the most important country roads were traced, parallel to the rivers from which shorter roads branched perpendicularly: the whole pattern presents an orthogonal network from the fifteenth century in the Upper-Argens plain, from the eighteenth or nineteenth century in the drainage zones of the marshes (*palus*) and the sub-littoral depressions.

Parts of these rural roads, improved and used again, are found in the layout of modern roads and even within cities in the pattern of their oldest streets. In Paris, certain streets, like the Faubourg Saint-Honoré probably correspond to pre-Roman routes.

The persistence of these layouts is assured not only by the stability of the division (even after the regrouping of land, very often the large plots have been delimited based on the old network and the same is true for urban blocks of houses (*îlots*) corresponding to plots or to the consolidations of rural plots) but also by their very structure: often cobbled or paved, almost always raised above the furrows or even, in the *bocage* regions, emphasized by ditches and embankments with hedgerows. A good number of these old roads, functioning as lines of communication from village to village or from hamlet to farm, or from an access route to a group of fields, to a forest skirt, still subsist and frequently form the boundaries of cadastral sections. Their origin explains their layout which is needlessly twisted, even in the plains, because they were moulded around fields already parcelled out and around existing properties, detouring to serve this or that formerly important point. Others, on the contrary, are improperly straight, spanning slopes and valleys without regard for a topography that is sometimes rather undulating: such as the famous *chaussées Brunehaut* in northern France, which now often link small market towns of trifling importance, but which were layed out in the Gallo-Roman period by the occupying forces concerned about distant and rapid communications, and whose horse-drawn vehicles were refractory to sudden and repeated turnings.

Belonging to the community, these routes became arteries of major communication, local or departmental roadways, so numerous and so well maintained (regularly paved with broken stone and often tarred) and which make France the best served country in the world in terms of secondary roads.

Land use

Many factors have played a subtle role in the conditions of land use. Among them are: physical environment, historical evolution, the development of economic facilities — particularly the organization of transportation and the proximity to or distance from centres of consumption, the nature of their demands — as well as the change, more or less developed, of rural outlooks.

General statistics indicate the relative importance of the major classical categories for the entire country. In total, 33.9 per cent of the land is arable, 24 per cent comprises various types of grassland cover, 20.7 per cent is woodlands and forests, 7.8 per cent uncultivated agricultural land, 2.7 per cent vineyards, 1.8 per cent truck farming, orchards, kitchen gardens, etc. This distribution is not fixed: since the beginning of the twentieth century, the area of arable land has decreased by more than 10 per cent, and that of vineyards by 0.5 per cent, whereas, on the contrary, the area of wooded lands has increased by 3.2 per cent and that of pastureland by 4.7 per cent. Regional combinations likewise vary greatly from one end of the country to the other. As it is not possible to make a detailed analysis of all these distributions, we have once again tried to summarize the characteristics of some of the major types (Pinchemel, 1969, 261).

Forest

Originally, the forest was the most widespread form of natural vegetation in France. Conditions were favourable in many respects: moisture from the oceanic climate of the west where forests of oak and beech alternated with coverings of aspen, birch, ash and pine, and in damp clearings with elder, willow and alder; moisture and coolness of the western mountain slopes of the Vosges, Jura, Pre-Alps, the main ranges of the northern Alps, Limousin, Auvergne, and the western Pyrenees; soil types, too, such as the sandstone of the Lorraine plateau, the clayey sands composed of eroded material brought down from the neighbouring mountains such as the sands of Périgord (*sidérolithique*), and those that fill a part of peripheral basins of the Central Massif in the Boischaut in Berry, around the Morvan, and in Sologne. Even the environs of Paris must have been largely wooded — except for the *limon* tablelands of the plateaux — and perhaps even the Causses, whose extreme aridity has been attributed by some to the depredations of man and especially of sheep (Roupnel, 1932).

The regression of the forest cover has been neither regular nor uniform. Its extent is the result of an equilibrium between natural conditions, man's needs, and his technology: generally over the centuries, peaceful eras maintained the forest, whereas periods of crisis favoured its extension. Indeed, for a long time, the ability of the forest to conquer the land and the possibilities of the rural population to limit its growth appeared to be unequal. The retreat of wooded areas was linked with three factors: systematic clearing and burning to extend cultivated lands; utilization for pasture first by pigs which caused little damage, then by the devastating sheep; finally, its exploitation for lumber, fuel, industrial, raw material.

The first major efforts to clear the forests began in prehistoric times with the adoption of a sedentary way of life by certain tribes, the cultivation of grain, and the use of metal tools: the axe became the auxiliary of fire in clearing the land. This continued during the Roman occupation and expanded in the Middle Ages with the increase in population, notably under the impetus of the great abbeys and Carolingian domains during the seventh and eighth centuries, the great Cluniac monasteries of the eleventh century and Cistercian monasteries of the twelfth century. The Cistercians are reputed to have been the greatest land clearers in historic times; establishing their abbeys in solitary, wooded and often humid areas, they replaced forest with pasture. In the same period, villagers were clearing their land, and collectively exploiting the forest. After a break in and a renewal of afforestation during long and itinerant wars such as the Hundred Years War throughout the west, and the Thirty Years War in the northeast, the eighteenth century then witnessed the emergence of a great period of mastery over the forest domain: vast clearings in geometric shapes and with characteristic names developed. These were then partially abandoned during the nineteenth century and especially in the twentieth century as a result of rural depopulation. A new stage began with voluntary reforestation, the best example of which is the Landes planted in the nineteenth century and today the most beautiful artificial national forest, but many others could be cited such as the Cevennes, the Morvan, etc. A mere wandering through the mountains and even the plains, as in Champagne, is sufficient to see the dark, massive and regular layout of black Austrian pines. Their extension is evidence of a trend which, with the use of wood for more and more numerous purposes (paper, cellulose, etc.) besides its traditional uses, is more and more prevalent and more and more profitable.

However, some regions have been so affected by the devastation of forest land and natural conditions are such, that, up to now at least, it has been impossible to reforest. Thus in the southern Alps or the Languedoc *garrigues*, the trees were cleared to plant grain fields and vineyards, sometimes on slopes where the soil was poor and soon exhausted or even eroded by the heavy rains of the Mediterranean climatic regime. From the thirteenth to the sixteenth centuries, vineyards clung to almost all the hillsides of the valleys in southern Dauphine and in Upper Provence. In other places, flocks of sheep and goats, belonging not only to local landowners but also to those of neighbouring areas climbed along the 'drove-roads' (*drailles*) to places of high elevation, grazing ruthlessly on scanty grass, on brushwood, and on young shoots. From the fifteenth century, in the southern Alps, a sort of cattle community was created where the herds were much too numerous for the available pasture. Moreover, in the winter, the peasants stripped the leaves and cut the branches from white oaks in order to mix them with straw and feed the local herd. Lacking straw they used boxwood. The forest was unable to withstand such treatment. In the case of the Languedoc *garrigues* their proximity to the cities, which are great consumers of wood, added its own consequences to the vicissitudes of the rural exploitation: from the Middle Ages to the seventeenth and eighteenth centuries, the price of wood rose steadily. On the eve of the French Revolution, there were no longer any real forests in the *garrigue* of Montpellier, and it was even found necessary to move certain related activities, such as the glass industry, to the mountain lands where in 40 years the Larzac woods were wiped out. A certain form of *garrigue* economy had been established; once it was ruined in the second half of the nineteenth century, particularly by the destruction of the vineyards, the forest proved incapable of recovering lost ground, except in the case of a few local pine forests (Dugrand, 1964, 292; Sclafert, 1934, 126—45).

Heath and wastelands

Heath and wastelands occupy a rather large percentage of the territory. They share in common the fact that they have both been totally neglected by man, but their history is different. The heathlands may always have been abandoned; they have sometimes followed after a rash clearing project or an unconsidered exploitation of the forest. They cover infertile and wind-swept summits, as in the hills of Brittany or the Millevaches Plateau they may also extend over plateaux covered with quasi-sterile sands as in the *landes* of Ruchart, on the plateaux which flank the Loire valley. Furze, broom, heather and bracken compete for their poor soil and adorn them with gold in spring or purple in summer. The wastelands, on the other hand, display all the melancholy of lands which were at one time cultivated and have now been forsaken by man: broken fences, crumbling terraces, plants returned to their wild state. Naturally it is not the best lands which have been abandoned in this way, but rural depopulation has had a considerable influence on the choices which have been made and the general low density of the French population is also a major factor in the development of this type of landscape, whose area doubled in the course of the past century. For a long time, certain geographers, economists and politicians were troubled by this insidious advance of the wastelands, considering them to be the evidence of an insufficient French population and a kind of renunciation. A more accurate view of the situation now prevails: it is better to concentrate one's efforts on the best lands whose yields continually increase and to abandon those which demand too much effort for too meagre a return. Part of these lands, generally located in mountainous regions, will undoubtedly be reforested or else will be included within the borders of national or regional parks currently in the process of being created in many French regions.

Grasslands

Grassland areas are likewise making important progress, especially in the most humid regions where they are better suited to the natural conditions than are cultivated crops, and in those regions where the withdrawal of the rural population has been accompanied by a great increase in stock farming. These grasslands are of very different types: three-quarters of them are permanent grasslands, whose quality is far from excellent. They occupy the land because nothing else would grow there. 'All these degenerated meadows and pasturelands which now languish exposing their rocks, their ant-hills, their thickets . . .', such is the picture painted by Lucien Gachon who at the same time points out that in Normandy or in certain particularly well-watered mountains as Savoy, the Jura, Cantal, the Mont-Dore, etc., the meadowlands, nevertheless, do offer possibilities. On the other hand, the artificial meadowlands and temporary meadowlands which represent approximately one-quarter of the grassland areas are the object of careful attention and represent an undeniable source of rural wealth. However, the system whereby on the same lands are alternated a certain number of years of cultivation followed by a certain number of years of meadowlands is relatively uncommon in France and involves hardly more than 1 million out of the 18 million hectares of grasslands.

The distribution of the meadowlands is just about the reverse of that of arable lands: they predominate in western France, where the department of La Manche holds a kind of record (63.4 per cent of the total area; the area of grassland has more than quadrupled since 1850), in the Central Massif, where Cantal and Lozère are likewise more than half covered by grassland, and in the humid mountainous regions. But even in the heart of cultivated regions, certain patches of grassland stand out: Thiérache, the district of Bray, Woëvre humid Champagne, eastern Normandy, etc. On the other hand in the Mediterranean districts, in view of the climatic conditions, meadowland disappears almost completely.

But throughout these grasslands the characteristics vary widely: rich meadows with thick, abundant grasses in western Normandy with its impermeable soils and moist climate, in the Nivernais, in the Charolais on the heavy clay soils of the Lias; shorter grass, which is nevertheless still good enough for cattle and even to reap on the meadowlands covering the well-watered hills and the crystalline plateaux of the Limousin; pastures luxuriant in the spring but soon withered stretching as far as the eye can see on the high ridges of the Central Massif; mountain pastures now almost completely abandoned on the high Alpine slopes.

Vineyards

Spread over a small area that has decreased by nearly one-fifth since the beginning of this century, vineyards occupy a place in the economic life, and especially in the preoccupations of the French people, which has no bearing on their area. This valuable crop seems to have been introduced into France as early as the sixth century B.C. from Greece via Central Europe: the first vineyards prospered on the well-exposed slopes of the Burgundy hills. They began to spread out in the Roman period with the growth of trade routes, then the Catholic liturgy, requiring the use of ritual wine for mass further contributed to its wide dispersion throughout all of France, where it was almost ubiquitous up until the eighteenth century. Every village had its own plots of vineyards whose yields were as poor as their cultivation was difficult. Important vineyards prospered only near the sea and the ports, as for example that of the Bordelais (Bordeaux region), enlarged in the twelfth century and transformed into an export wine industry that served England, and the countries of the Hanseatic League. 'This vine held such an important place in the lives of our ancestors, that any person of rank among them, cultivated it for honor as much as for profit' (Dion, 1959, 768; Marres, 1950, 224).

Thus human conditions have figured as much as the natural environment in the distribution of French vineyards. It has been possible to show the relationship between the extension of the vineyards with the index of aridity for July: if it is high, vineyards can spread out broadly on the plains, as in the case of the great vineyards of Aquitaine or of those in the Mediterranean regions; if it is low, their extent must be limited to the well-exposed southern and south-eastern hillsides, as in Champagne, Burgundy, the Loire regions and Alsace.

Since the latter half of the nineteenth century, the French wine industry has undergone profound upheavals: the effects of the phylloxera blight brought about important changes in the localization and notably in the creation of a monoculture in Languedoc; the development of transportation permitting specialization resulted in the disappearance of a certain number of marginal vineyards. At present, the vine is not found in France beyond a line passing from the Loire estuary on the west, including the slopes of the Loir valley, passing south of the Paris region, north of Champagne and of the Moselle hills. In all, seventeen departments no longer have vineyards. However, in only six departments does the vine cover more than 28 per cent of the usable agricultural land (Hérault, eastern Pyrenees, Var, Gironde, Aude and Gard). Current policy favours the voluntary uprooting of vines and the more mediocre the wine, the higher the compensation is for the owner; new areas cannot be planted unless a prior uprooting of old stock is proven. This, however, does not affect the vintage wines, whose yield is insufficient (particularly in Champagne and Burgundy), while the surplus production of ordinary table wines makes diversification in land use desirable, especially in Languedoc (Lombard, 1951, 146).

Rural settlements

Settlement is an essential element of the rural landscape. Its variety is evident at once in the general layout of the dwellings, the particular structure of the groups of buildings, the house styles, the materials used. The French territory affords such diversity that it is necessary to limit our comments to a few characteristic features.

Distribution and evolution

The population is very evenly distributed throughout the country. Very few regions appear devoid of buildings: the mountain heights are without them above 900 m (2953 ft) in Limousin, above 1000 m (3281 ft) in Vivarais, and above 1850 m (6070 ft) in the southern Alps, where Saint Véran is one of the highest villages in Europe; poor soils, even in the plains, are almost abandoned: there are fewer than six rural inhabitants per square kilometre in the Landes of the Aquitaine basin.

But certain areas are quite well supplied with buildings and yet empty of people, either because the dwelling units were temporary, associated with the annual cycles of stock raising, as in the 'mountains' (chalets situated high up for the summering either of livestock or of the inhabitants and the flocks in the Alps or in the heart of the Central Massif), or because of the extensive and prolonged emigration, a veritable rural 'exodus' which has deprived the villages and the hamlets of the majority — and sometimes the totality — of their residents. This depopulation of mountain communities generally began not long before the beginning of the nineteenth century; it caused the mountains of Corsica, the southern Alps, the northern Pre-Alps, and the high valleys of the main ranges of the northern Alps to lose two-thirds of their population, the market towns of Cevennes to lose three-quarters since 1910 (and the ruin of silkworm breeding), and some hamlets in the Causses and Haute Auvergne to lose the totality of their populations. Everywhere houses built of resistant stone subsist; their walls stand more or less intact with caved in roofs amid fields of brambles and nettles. A few elderly people remain there, living out their final years. Sometimes urban families buy houses deserted by rural dwellers, decorate them, landscape them, and spend their leisure-time there. In this way, villages around the large cities are being preserved and renovated. Acquisition of such second homes by Parisians occurs in an area that extends from Picardy to Sologne and from Morvan to Normandy; those of the residents of Marseille are located throughout the hills of Provence and the hinterland of the Mediterranean coves as far as the massif of Maures; the residents of Lyons, Saint-Etienne and Grenoble penetrate the eastern part of the Central Massif, the northern part of the Alps and the southern borders of the Jura. Some hilltop villages of inland Provence are now the object of a veritable recolonization on the part of French people from all parts of the country.

Nucleated and dispersed settlement

Even a cursory examination of the rural landscapes shows the contrast of two markedly different types: the nucleated dwelling pattern with the houses crowded more or less tightly together within a quite strictly defined area; the dispersed dwelling pattern where the houses are isolated from one another. The Lorraine village and the farms of coastal Flanders serve as characteristic examples of these two, almost schematic, types.

But it would be foolhardy to conclude from this that the types are easy to classify. All intermediate forms are represented, and, though it is possible to discern generally areas of clustered dwellings, broadly corresponding to openfield areas, and areas of very scattered dwellings, freely dispersed in districts of *bocage*, all the nuances do exist. In

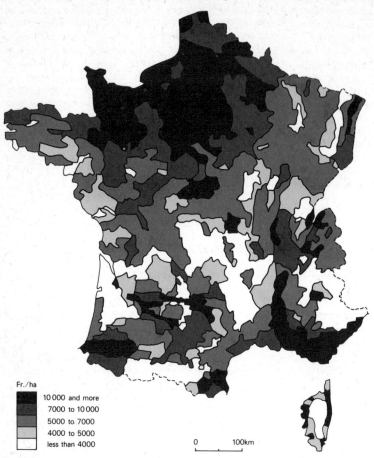

Fr./ha
10 000 and more
7000 to 10 000
5000 to 7000
4000 to 5000
less than 4000

0   100km

Fig. 7   Price of arable land in 1970. (The limits are those of agricultural regions)

general, however, what characterizes a rural settlement pattern as opposed to an urban one, is its repetitive reproduction, or one could say, its regular pattern of homogeneous elements: these elements can be villages that are more or less important, more or less loosely grouped, houses made up of more or less disparate elements, or houses and villages in alternation.*

Nucleated settlement consists of villages, either aligned along a single street, or spread out along several intersecting roads giving the effect of massive or star-shaped groupings. Lorraine provides many examples of

* Elements are more fully described in Juillard *et al.*, 1957; Derruau, 1949; Lebeau, 1955; Livet, 1962; Bloch, 1951; Dion, 1934, 1946. For the simplified classification used here, refer to Demangeon (1946/1948), vol. 1, pp. 166–215.

all these types; in Lower-Provence, the size of the market-town, cramped wall against wall and conserving the same concentration of grouped life, may characterize even hamlets.

In certain instances, the rural dwelling pattern may be *grouped* without being compact. In Picardy, villages occur in valley hollows and in folds of the relief, sheltered from the winds and escaping the dryness of the chalky plateau, real bouquets of greenery where brick houses are encircled by a grassy enclosure planted with apple trees. In the Pays de Caux, similar farms in their grassy enclosures line the highways and roadways, sometimes for kilometres at a stretch: they are related to former forest clearings of the late Middle Ages, such as near the Lillebonne forest.

Dispersed settlement corresponds to a scattering of human groups which in the extreme is represented by an isolated farm amid its own lands, such as is found in the rolling hills of the centre of the Aquitaine basin, in the plains of Maritime Flanders, in the higher regions of the eastern-central Jura or in eastern Velay. In this type of complete dissociation, the centre of the commune itself is scattered: the church, town hall, school, and shops may be separated. However, most frequently four or five farms group together constituting scattered hamlets, of which one, more important, is the centre that gives its name to the commune. Frequently these hamlets bear names disclosing their origin, posterior to the main nuclei: names such as 'Les Essarts' (clearings), 'Les Brûlés' (burnt-over areas) reflecting the medieval destruction of forest land, 'La Folie' (madness), 'les Droits de l'Homme' (the rights of man) echoing the eighteenth century, or with a patronymic recalling the establishment of a family branch such as the Garnier's, the Pages's, the Ripert's, the Bardin's. Members of the same family added their own buildings over a period of time, then pushed a little farther on. With rural depopulation, the reverse process has taken place: a single family taking over all the best buildings in the hamlet. These types and their fluctuations are found in Limousin and in western Armorica: a scattering of hamlets (as many as 25 or more in one commune), distribution of hamlets with farms interspersed.

Mixed settlement associates nuclei more or less tightly grouped and an interspersed scattering of isolated dwellings. Such a pattern had already emerged in certain regions by the end of the Middle Ages, adding to the central market town the inhabitants of the peripheral clearings; the modern version of this type is well developed on the plains of Lower-Rhône and Provence. There, for reasons of security or health (risks of Saracen attack along the coasts, choice of elevated sites where observation and defence were easier, sometimes also risks of malaria in the poorly drained plains), villages with tall, narrow houses and visible stone walls were in the past squeezed in the summits of hills. With the improvement of security and the development of the lands, attractive modern houses were constructed in many places, each one settling close to his own plot of land. This dispersion was fostered by the types of crops — truck-farming, fruit trees, flowers — requiring a daily presence and care at all hours, thus close proximity was desirable. Hilltop villages, if they are not sufficiently picturesque and well

57

situated to be sought after by the purchasers of a second home, are largely abandoned because of the difficulties of access and practicability of the road.

House types and building materials

To these types of structures which recur throughout France and which may reflect local conditions as much as different eras, there must be added the regional character of our villages. Throughout France have existed true local house types: two peasants practising the same kind of farming in Poitou and in Lorraine, in Beauce and in Aquitaine, did not build their farms in the same way. A further consideration was the dependence on the local materials. In contrast to the more powerful and better organized town, which at least for its public buildings could order special materials from greater distances, the villages were obliged to find on the spot what they needed for construction.

Albert Demangeon, the great geographer to whom the human geography of France is greatly indebted, proposed a classification of rural houses by major categories, which are both morphological and functional at the same time. It can be quoted, but it gives a rather schematic and rigid idea of the extreme actual diversity. He has distinguished 'block-houses' where the peasant family, the cattle, the agricultural implements and the harvested crops are housed under a single roof. This 'block' dwelling may be horizontal lying close to the earth, juxtaposing the family dwelling and the farm building, as in Brittany or in south-central France; or it can be wide, massive, almost quadrangular, with a second storey, as in the deep Lorraine house; or a tall house superimposing stable or storeroom, family quarters, a loft for harvested crops, as in Mediterranean-Midi, in the southern part of the Central Massif, in the Rhône valley and its borders: the dwellings of the wine-growers represent this type *par excellence*. At the opposite extreme, 'houses with separate buildings' have many variants: buildings arranged in a square around a farmyard completely closed towards the outside, as in the large farms of the centre of the Paris basin; buildings are spaced some distance from each other, but nevertheless forming a kind of 'open farmyard', as are frequently found in western France, in Berry, and in Sologne, and a third type sometimes arranged in a much more disorderly way in the heart of a green enclosure where a few apple trees grow, as in the Pays de Caux (Demangeon, 1946/1948; Faucher, 1945, 241–53).

Thus exteriorly, the Breton rural settlement pattern has nothing in common with the Alsatian village. The Breton village has low houses of grey granite, roofed with slate, continued by the grey pattern of the low dry walls which border the fields, while the Alsatian village has white-washed plastered walls with cross-timbering painted in sombre colours, high red-tiled roofs, and its windows decorated with flower-pots. In the villages of Picardy and of the north the houses are of red brick, set against the greenery of the yards and of the trees. The farm-houses of Lorraine, Burgundy, and Poitou are built of square, small blocks of local limestone that are sometimes golden and sometimes greyish, always very square and securely sheltered under their red roofs.

In the Jura, the rural dwelling takes on a severe but majestic capaciousness under a strong roof under which dry the heavy ears of golden corn. In the southern part of the Central Massif and in Provence, the house rises, narrow, clinging to the harsh features of the relief, its thick stone walls barely pierced by narrow windows, on a rocky foundation hardly distinguishable from the walls; it is covered by an almost flat roof of rounded tiles, orange coloured or almost white, bleached by the sun.

There is in all these old dwellings a certain tang of the earth, and a naive architecture which is enhanced by the local churches, often inspired by the great religious edifices of neighbouring towns. These churches are small in their dimensions, but remarkable for the harmony of their proportions, the beauty of the stonework, and the admixture of styles, revealing centuries of religious fervour on the part of communities which were poor and few in numbers, but faithful.

Alongside this provincialism of the past, are appearing new buildings, even in the villages. These are built by retired people returning to their birthplace or by modern, enterprising cultivators, who can no longer put up with the uncomfortable family home, or by townsfolk seeking to be near the fields, whether in a permanent residence, or in a second, vacation home for weekends or holidays. Many are having houses built in a style which is too often the impersonal one-family house, or, what is scarcely an improvement, houses in recognizable styles, belonging to other regions. High mountain chalets of varnished wood can thus be seen even in the area around Paris or on the sea coasts; imitation Norman houses are found under all skies, and as far as the Mediterranean coast. Finally, in areas devastated by the wars, such as Normandy in 1944, there are entire rural centres which have been rebuilt in residential houses of the urban type, all the farm buildings removed to the periphery amidst the lands under cultivation. Consequently, the rural dwelling pattern is assuming a new profile, possibly more rational, more comfortable for the inhabitants, and more in keeping with the modern tendencies toward uniformity. But alas they are much less characteristic of regional life!

4
Some examples of rural landscapes*

All the elements described in the previous chapter are combined in various ways, and it is perhaps useful to conclude by sketching a few portraits of the existing rural landscapes.

The *Flemish countryside* is divided in two by the completely artificial Franco—Belgian border. Composed of heavy clay soils in a damp climate, these lands have been improved by intensive human effort and a considerable quantity of fertilizer; the careful attention lavished upon these fields was facilitated by a large and prolific population which was increased by hard-working foreign immigrants. The population lives on medium-sized family farms. In the midst of fields of wheat, of sugar-beets and potatoes having the highest yields in France are found more specialized crops as hops, flax, etc., that used to be more widespread. Openfields and hedgerows alternate according to the locality: bare in the centre and on the Artois hills, the plain has more trees and takes on a green colour south of the regular grid pattern of the coastal polders, or as one ascends the first hills of the Pre-Ardennes. The villages are brick, ground level, dense and monotonous; toward the south, as in eastern Picardy, the sugar refineries construct their large industrial buildings and high chimneys in the midst of fields under cultivation. In maritime Flanders, the former oast-houses are still common near the farms and old abandoned mills raise their useless towers. Roads, railroads and canals have dense networks with heavy traffic, especially between the coal district, the conurbation of Lille—Roubaix—Tourcoing and the sea. This landscape already announces the intense land use of the Netherlands and is linked with the great industrial zone of the Rhine.

In the heart of the *Paris basin*, surrounding the vast complex of the Paris agglomeration which reaches out its tentacles along the valleys and the great axes of communication, the Tertiary plateaux of Beauce, of Brie, of Valois and of Soissonnais stretch out in vast tablelands generally covered with *limon* and gently undulating, where trees are rare, gathered in geometric copses or small woods, which are the refuge of wild game. These are cereal lands *par excellence*, and have long been considered the granaries of France; depending on the type of *limon* soils, the proximity to the centre of consumption and of processing, these plateaux also carry sugar-beets, potatoes, field vegetables, etc.

* For more detailed descriptions of this subject see Chabot, 1969.

Recently, especially in Beauce, these crops have been replaced by corn as the chief crop. During the season when there is a sea of ripe wheat waving in the breeze, the green of the corn has changed the appearance of the countryside, as have the drying-lofts, long narrow grills placed on well-aerated ridges and filled up every winter with ears of golden corn. The fields are very large, in fact huge by French standards, as the result of a vigorous programme to regroup the lands. The farms increase in size while they diminish in number because of rural depopulation: the largest exceeds 200 hectares. Mechanization is very prevalent and perhaps even superabundant: it is not uncommon to count two tractors on a farm of 25 hectares. The optimum is a farm of 50 to 100 hectares, cultivated by a farmer and his wife, and occasionally aided by a relative or neighbour to whom the same service is rendered. The consumption of fertilizer is high and constantly increasing; the yields are likewise increasing and exceed 60 quintals of wheat per hectare in good years. Commercialization is very modern. In the hands of powerful grain-storage cooperatives or wealthy private merchants, grain elevators, often recently built, dominate the plains with their massive towers, just like the water towers and church steeples, some of which are admirable examples of Roman or Gothic architecture, using the resources of local limestone quarries. These high buildings indicate at a distance the presence of nucleated villages, which are outlined as well by the foliage of the trees. In these market towns, the large, solidly built farmhouses with square farmyards, which are sometimes also found isolated in the midst of their fields, look like fortresses shut off from the outside and opened on to their courtyards enclosed by farm buildings; these large farmhouses alternate with the small dwellings of artisans, agricultural workers, or peasants, the majority of whom are now disappearing or ageing and their vacant dwellings are becoming second homes, bedecked with flowers and renovated by Parisians avid for rural tranquillity. Cattle, always relatively scarce, are in the process of disappearing. In Beauce, the stables are empty; the farmer's wife buys her milk and butter at the more or less distant supermarket; she travels by car, in the same way as her husband commutes to work in the fields; after the harvest, some close down the farm and go away on vacation, leaving the countryside to vacationers from the cities. The land has thus become a raw material, and agriculture an industry like any other.

A sea of greenery envelops *western Normandy*: the moist, oceanic climate, the impermeable nature of the ancient, crystalline and primary rocks of the Armorican Massif planed down to rows of low hills, the surface decomposition of the argillaceous rocks — all these contribute to make this region the domain of grass and trees. They are ubiquitous: thick, verdant meadows, where the grass grows throughout the year, enclosed by hedgerows dotted with apple trees, broken by small woods, interrupted by extensive forests located on the most infertile soils or on the hillsides that are crowned above 300 m (985 ft) with heath and broom moors. Yet interruptions in this verdant landscape begin to appear: to obtain better profits, the hedgerows are being abolished and the apple trees cut down; they are being replaced by well-maintained orchards, producing good eating apples instead of the small apples that

61

are only good for making the famous cider and an alcohol called *calva*, which is drunk locally a little too generously, to the detriment of the population's health.

Farmhouses are small, concealed in the greenery and often located at some distance from one another. Previously, houses had thatched roofs whose ridges were bedecked with flowers, but today roofing is more prosaic, generally slate or tile. The buildings are smaller because there is neither shelter for the cattle, nor for the crops, but only for the family and some farm implements. In fact, this region is entirely devoted to stock-raising in the open air. The herd of dairy cattle or young bovines being fattened spend all their time outdoors, gorging themselves on the grass which never stops growing; the milking is done mechanically on the spot; the milk is collected in sterilized cans deposited by trucks belonging to the local cooperatives who then come to collect the cans and transport the precious liquid to factories, where it is sterilized, pasteurized, and shipped to Paris and other big cities in large refrigerated tanks, or else preserved (powdered milk, evaporated milk), or even made into butter and cheese. This region, rich in meat and in dairy products, where some villages carry the names of famous cheeses (Camembert, Pont-l'Evêque), is orientated essentially to stock-raising, and it has been said in jest that the day when the cows could milk themselves, the peasant of western Normandy would have nothing more to do!

The *coastal plain of Léon*, a wide peninsula on the north-western tip of Brittany, enjoys a still more perfect oceanic climate. Its regular, moist mildness, reinforced by the passage along its coast of a warm, tropical ocean current — the Gulf Stream — assures this bank of ancient erosion surfaces, which wore down the crystalline rocks, exceptional climatic conditions. Here frost and snow are almost unknown; a rich *limon*, further improved by the continual addition of marine fertilizers which are fetched from the beaches and transported by tipcarts to the tiny fields (calcareous mud made up of fragments of shells crushed by the sea and algae that have been torn up from the bottom of the sea by the waves and left to decay before being ploughed under), is well utilized by a large population (120 inhabitants per sq km) where a solid, rural Roman Catholic tradition has long sustained a high birthrate. These farms are much too small, so despite their intensive methods of cultivation, the returns are inadequate, especially as the remarkable increase in production during the last twenty years has caused a terrible slump in prices which accounts for the dissatisfaction of the Bretons who demand a better lot. In a group of square fields that are as small as gardens, two to three crops are harvested annually (early potatoes, cauliflower, onions, peas, artichokes). Saint-Pol-de-Léon is one of the centres of the commercialization of this production. The grey granite houses with slate roofs and fronts that are painted white each year, are so low that they seem to sink down into the ground in order to be sheltered from the wind. Many young people and even entire families, encouraged by the Ministry of Agriculture, are leaving the hamlets to go and settle in the sparsely populated areas of the Aquitaine basin or the south-eastern part of the Paris basin where they can occupy family farms that are three or four times larger. Fishing, not long ago a family enterprise carried on in every little creek, is on the decline, because of the industrialization necessitating much larger boats, more sheltered harbours and considerably more capital. As for the tourist trade, it is restricted to from six weeks to two months (July—August), too brief a period to permit any really profitable organization. This region — so beautiful — is one of those needing the greatest attention for its economic development.

On the high crystalline plateaux isolated *in the heart of the Central Massif* (Limousin, Auvergne), the population has become sparse. The inhabitants have been rebuffed by the harsh climatic conditions (snow from six weeks to three months each year), by the infertile soil which spontaneously would be the domain of a beautiful forest, or on the summits a heathland, but which has been repeatedly deforested under demographic pressure, from the Middle Ages until the eighteenth century, and which now barely supports a few meagre food crops scattered with broken stones, or permanent pastures poorly maintained when it is not returned to wasteland, that is to say abandoned. Thus many people have left: villages have lost half their population in a century, and only old people or single people are left behind in moribund villages. A hamlet that once long ago sheltered four or five families now has only one, which has taken over the best buildings while the others fall into ruin or become overgrown with vegetation. Sombre and dry stone is found everywhere: in the piles of stones which separate the tiny parcels, where the practice of regrouping the land has not yet penetrated; in the rural dwellings with thick walls, roofed with square tiles or sombre plates of schist (*lauzes*); in large vertical stone blocks staked out so that the traveller of days gone by might find his way across the snow-covered and wind-swept wilderness. A harsh, austere and majestic region spreads its large coniferous forests whose red trunks plunge into the savage gorges of the valleys which fragment the plateau and have sometimes been blocked by the great dams, transforming them into a series of lakes, such as the Creuse at Eguzon, the Dordogne all along its upper course. To cross these valleys there are many famous bridges and viaducts: Garabit, having the same iron framework as the Eiffel Tower, the viaduct of Fades, one of the first great works of this type in concrete. The villages are often broken up into hamlets using the sheltered shelves where a little fertile soil is spread out. The livestock lives shut up during the winter in warm, dim stables; in the summer it comes out into the meadows next to the village, during the day, in small individual herds of a few head, or else is gathered together into a collective herd to go up to the pasturelands in the mountains (Aubrac, Cantal). The summits have been rounded by long periods of erosion and cut up by valleys that are senile and flat because they have been filled up by debris which slipped down from the slopes; these slopes, already very smooth in the periglacial period, are denuded: landes (see p. 52) of heather or furze, perennial bracken, which invades the fallowlands and the underbrush, give way to vast areas of short grass containing a few peat-bogs with dark sombre waters in the humid hollows. Many peasants, who have been leaving the soil for a century and who today are still leaving it, have become 'Parisians' but they return to their native region for vacation and sometimes for retirement.

The *centre of the Aquitaine basin*, on the two banks of the Garonne, between the region of Toulouse to the east and that of Bordeaux to the west, is one of the most surprising of the French regions, Hills, somewhat formless and yet sharp-pointed, carved out of thick Tertiary terrains that are almost uniquely sandstone, have furnished man, seemingly, with reasonable conditions: a soil not stripped of fertility, a climate mild in the winter, warm and sufficiently watered in the summer. However, the region has difficulty in retaining its inhabitants: depopulated for the first time near the beginning of the twentieth century, she received contingents of peasants from Brittany and the Central Massif, who were leaving unfavourable areas in search of better lands; the tremendous hecatombs of the First World War deprived her of a large part of her young men, and in the years that followed, it was necessary to call upon an official immigration of Italian families to assure the maintenance of the farms. These Italians in turn left the villages in great number because of the vicissitudes in Franco–Italian relations during the course of the second international conflict. Today, the families of repatriates from North Africa, first from Morocco, then Algeria after 1961, have taken root in this region. How can we understand this recent history? It is enough to look at a map. Dwellings are very dispersed, situated from one hill to the next; human consequences: the people are isolated; material consequences: for a long time, in fact, up until these last few years, there was neither water, nor electricity in the buildings, because of the high costs of installing electric lines and water lines; finally, the large cities are far away, local centres, like Agen, are poorly equipped and the rural inhabitants flee this quasi-desert. The new arrivals, the *pieds-noirs* (Algerians of European origin), are trying to revive the region. They do not fear the isolation and are accustomed to the hard work that goes along with difficult ventures. The traditional mixed farming associates cereals (wheat, corn) with orchards of fruit trees (plums of Agen) and vineyards: it is the most famous region in France for table grapes (Moissac, whose well-known name comes from the small town that is also known for its magnificent abbey). In place of small farms, where the regrouping of land is just about beginning, and where share-cropping is still in practice, the newcomers substitute the large, well-equipped domain under direct development by buying back the parcels; they plunge into arboriculture, fruit production, and stock-raising on a large scale; they renovate dwellings. Will their sporadic presence succeed in overthrowing the kind of curse which seems to loom over the region?

For *Alsace*, we could sketch a portrait which would be exactly the reverse of the preceding one. A small north–south plain, well-defined between the sombre forests of the Vosges to the west and the broad humid Rhine valley to the east, it is almost perfectly flat, fragmented by the former terraces into three scarcely perceptible tiers, the two highest of which are covered by a thick and fertile *loess*. Partly sheltered from oceanic influences by the Vosges, but receiving precipitation from summer storms resulting from continental influences, Alsace is moderately watered. Along with the Breton coasts of the northwest and the Vaucluse region in the south, it is perhaps one of the French regions having the highest density of purely agricultural population. Large villages are numerous, with houses that are characterized by a visible brown painted framework supporting the whitewashed mud walls, and by windows decorated with cheerful flower-boxes: old villages that are still alive and active, surrounded by tiny and regular fields often still cultivated manually, where wheat, barley, potatoes, tobacco, cabbage, and hops grow; these hop-growing patches transform the landscape into clumps of geometric greenery. Near the Rhine, the humidity of the *rieds*, devoid of *limon*, is propitious to meadows and to patches of forest. To the west, on the slopes of the hills at the foot of the Vosges mountains the vineyard rises in tiers, dotted with most cheerful market towns, real little cities with monuments supported by pillars and sculptures of old red sandstone, coming from the Triassic cover of the northern Vosges.

Another type of privileged landscape is that part of the *plains of the Lower-Rhône* when the irrigation water brings its benefits and adds its advantages to those of a climate reputed for its warmth and sunshine in the summer and relative mildness in the winter. The Vauclusian plain is the most perfect example of this: waters coming from the Rhône, from the Durance, and from the Sorgue, flow in the branches of the irrigation canals. The land is priceless for growing early vegetables, flowers and famous fruits (Cavaillon melons, Isle-sur-Sorgue peaches, etc.) and the farms rarely exceed 2 or 3 hectares. Every night entire railroad freight cars and trucks filled with produce leave for Paris. Such crops require an abundant labour force; Italian and especially Spanish immigration has furnished large contingents of agricultural workers. The villages, formerly situated on the hills have moved down into the plain; the villagers have emigrated to innumerable new and attractive houses, distributed amid their cultivated lands. Prosperity reigns everywhere. A single shadow is cast: the *mistral*, a wind whose violent blast going down the Rhône valley can break trees and fragile plants; it is counteracted by the multiplication of hedges of cypress or of reeds, perpendicular to its direction, which literally chop up the landscape. As soon as one reaches the edge of the plains, terraces appear, planted with prosperous vineyards or abandoned olive trees. Thus, everywhere, in the regions bordering the Mediterranean, except in Languedoc where the plain is broader, tiny basins (Roussillon, Argens basin, Var basin, etc.) well-irrigated and well-cultivated contrast with the dry slopes of the hills that are sometimes terraced and sometimes covered with spoiled forests, such as *maquis* or *garrigue*.

It is necessary to make a place in these plains for a landscape that is rare in France, the rice fields. The *Camargue*, a large island that is half amphibious on its southern shores and whose lands surround the Vaccarès pond, forms a triangle between the arms of the larger-Rhône and the smaller-Rhône. People boast of the charm of its iridescent and wild horizons, of its herds of black bulls, raised for bullfights, of its light horses crossed with arab blood, of its flocks of pink flamingoes, but it is also a rich agricultural region. For a long time dedicated to wheat and to the vineyard, in its northern part which is the best drained, this region knew an important transformation during the course of the Second World War, when France, deprived of its connections with the exterior, and notably with Asian countries, its traditional rice suppliers, tried to produce on its own soil this cereal that is particularly indispensable to the sick and to children. Geometrically dug by powerful machines, the canals serve both to evacuate salt water into the Vaccarès pond, or into the Rhône, and to irrigate with fresh water at the right moment. It is not a question here of transplanting the rice, which would be too expensive, and consequently the rice beds are rapidly invaded by weeds; nevertheless half the French rice consumption can be produced with excellent yields. In order to house the rice cultivators (about 2000) without spoiling the beauty of the landscape, small white houses covered with reeds, very traditional in appearance and which hardly stand out on the alluvial plains, have been constructed.

The vineyard has its own landscapes. Sometimes it is integrated into a complex mixed farming scheme, in which it represents only one of the elements of the land use, as in the Bordeaux area, where it is found in the plains as well as along the hillsides or on the plateaux, around the châteaux bearing the names of the famous wines, or in the Loire region where it systematically hems the well-exposed slopes of the middle valley; sometimes, on the contrary, it constitutes the only source of wealth and dominates the entire landscape. Already marked in Burgundy on a narrow fringe, this predominance is affirmed in Languedoc, a land which has been known for its 'monoculture' for almost a century, the only classic example in France.

Along the *cuestas* of *Burgundy*, extend, as far as the eye can see, the vineyards belonging to numerous small landowners who lovingly care for them. The soil is almost artificial, so much have the additions in the course of the centuries transformed it: to the limestone substratum have been added the black earth from the plain by the wagonload, manure and fertilizers; each year, all the talus of the previous season has been patiently carried back up to the top of the field, that has been dug, cleared of stones, weeded. The stems of the vine are pruned short and supported by wooden vine props. How many generations have laboured on these slopes, which already had vineyards (near Autun, notably) way before the arrival of the Romans in Gaul? As a result excellent wines with multiple nuances, are produced in very limited quantity, sold either directly by the wine-growers, or by the wine-merchants for which Beaune and Nuits are the most famous capitals, without forgetting the nearby city of Dijon. The 'road of the wines' crosses nucleated villages, whose houses are built out of the local Burgundy stone, the famous golden limestone which sparkles in the sun; the houses are one storey high, above the cool and arched cellar, half buried, where the wine ages; as in Alsace, this road passes through all the famous wine-producing localities and is an important tourist attraction. A solid tradition of folklore and gastronomy is illustrated each year by the famous gatherings around the magnificent buildings of the Hospices de Beaune, or of the Clos-Vougeot.

Very different is the landscape of *Languedoc*. Here, the vineyard has overrun the entire region taking hold again after the phylloxera blight which, around 1875, destroyed, first of all this vineyard before ravaging the rest of France. The vine is found around ponds — occasionally with the stems in water for a few weeks each year — as well as on the sand beaches, on the interior plains, and even on the lower slopes of the limestone plateaux of the *garrigues*. About one-third of the lands belong to local townsmen who rent them to other people. The exploitations are fairly large, or else regrouped into cooperatives; also, the buildings for wine production are large, the villages grouped, with wine-growers' houses scattered in the heart of their fields. During the grape-gathering season, bands of Spaniards come to pick the grapes. The wine, generally low in alcohol content, must be blended with stronger wines, which for a long time had been imported from Algeria through the port of Sète. This monoculture is not without danger (repercussions of bad years, price slumps because of overproduction in good years), thus some attention has been given to the possibility of diversifying the crops. The irrigation canal of the Lower-Rhône—Languedoc, cut thanks to the *Société Mixte** of the same name, takes water from the smaller-Rhône and brings it to the heart of the vineyards; it has made it possible to develop corn fields and even, experimentally, cotton. Vegetable crops, orchards, especially apple trees, replace locally the uprooted vineyards. Along a belt bordering the canal, the cycle of monoculture is broken. A railway collecting point has been organized in Nîmes to permit the grouping and sale of the new products. This endeavour represents one of the positive efforts to develop the country ('*aménagement du territoire*', see pp. 30, 100).

The future of the French countryside

These few examples show that although French rural landscapes present an image of apparent stability, of a relative sclerosis because of the permanence of dwellings built very solidly, of the everlastingness of certain elements like roads, fences, etc., nevertheless the changes are profound. They are revealed externally for the observer sometimes through nuances that only a trained eye can perceive, or a precise investigation can reveal (reduction of the livestock or change in the types of stock-raising, internal changes in the use of buildings, electrification and generalized mechanization, plumbing installed in old buildings); sometimes, on the contrary, these changes are readily apparent even to the most untrained observer.

One of the most spectacular modifications of these last years is, of course, the redistribution of land, which has resulted in a simplification — sometimes remarkable — of the French agricultural land division. Attention should also be drawn to the disappearance of hedges in the *bocage* regions, which at the present time has almost transformed the Rennes basin into a vast openfield. The decrease in the number of farmers is also revealed by the concentration of farms: the very small

* A peculiar type of Company which associates public and private capital.

having less than 5 hectares dropped from 4 million in 1892 to a little more than 500 000 today. The number of farms of less than 10 hectares are also decreasing, while those which have from 10 to 20 and from 50 to 100 hectares are appreciably increasing. The farms in the 50 to 100 hectare range represent the most stable French type which permits a single family to cultivate its own land and draw from it the maximum profit. Finally, we note a certain increase in the farms of more than 100 hectares, corresponding to a veritable industrial type that is prevalent especially in the centre of the Paris basin. Other modifications are related to the crops themselves: corn has literally invaded the French territory and, at the present time, Beauce, the traditional wheat land, has become a vast green cornfield in the summer, since the creation of new hybrids enables it to brave the cooler and more northern climates. In the Midi, the new vines are planted in rows placed farther apart to facilitate the use of a motor-cultivator to work the land, and an even larger separation will be needed in order to use on a large scale the new machines which have just come into use for picking the grapes. The changes are rapid: sometimes they are real upheavals, and we can now conjure up the idea of a France without peasants, of a France with agricultural technicians — which seems to be a kind of a paradox considering the natural gifts and the past evolution of our country; but, even in this case, how many decades before all characteristics of traditional structure in the rural landscapes will disappear?

Nevertheless, the question has been asked: what will we do with the rural houses that have been so solidly built, how will we use the land when the French countrysides are emptied? Urban dwellers have already begun to answer. Many farms are transformed into vacation houses and entire villages come to life on weekends or during vacations, especially around the big cities and particularly in a region around Paris which extends as far as Sologne, the Morvan, western Normandy, the English Channel, and overlaps into the regions of Picardy and Champagne. In addition, we plan to conserve certain areas and protect them from the proliferation of construction as well as against any other attack of a modern, polluting, and disfiguring civilization: these are the national and regional parks, that are now being created in numerous French regions. Already the Vanoise Park has a great reputation in the Alps; another park will cover a large part of the Cevennes and tomorrow, why not, in other beautiful regions that have been abandoned by man such as the Central Massif, the southern Alps or even in the large forests of the Paris basin? It is often mentioned that France, relatively unpopulated in comparison with her neighbours, is perhaps one of the European countries with the brightest future in this domain, because she possesses what the men of tomorrow will lack the most: natural open space.

Part Three

The Urban Landscapes

Introduction

The idea of the 'town' suggests more modern images than that of the 'country'. However, in an old nation like France the urban network is the fruit of a long superposition. Each major historical period has left on its soil its share of towns created for diverse reasons, constructed according to very different needs, endowed with more or less bright futures. The necessity of defence, the need for meetings and exchanges, the requirements of government or administration, the aspiration for the calm of monastic life, the exploitation of natural resources, the use of modern technology, or just simply the growth of the population have all contributed to the burgeoning of cities, with more or less complex activities and diverse destinies within the French territory.

5
The major stages of urban development

The beginnings

From the prehistoric period in Gaul, urban concentrations existed in France. The colonies founded on the shores of the Mediterranean by Greek navigators are well known. The most famous is Massilia, offspring of the Phocaeans, founded in the sixth century B.C., using as a shelter one of the rocky coves of the Provençal coast: in 1965 the remains of this primitive port were found, proof of the birth of the second largest city in France today (Marseilles): 'A harbour close to the Rhône valley, that is to say the best access route from southern Europe, between the sea and the interior', toward the lands of this 'Gallic isthmus', already praised by Strabon (Pierrein, 1965, 149). From the fifth century B.C., this Massilia had already created colonies like Nice, Antibes, Agde, etc., removed never abandoned, ancestors of three of our coastal cities.

However, the Gauls themselves had already occupied and fortified certain areas, the famous *oppida* (towns); certain of these are now only excavation sites, or historical places with illustrious names, like Enserune, on the limestone plateaux of Languedoc, Gergovie, located on the volcanic hills which overlook Limagne, Alésia, whose exact site is still disputed ... but others have never ceased to exist. In certain regions of Gaul, it even seems that an embryo of urban development existed in the pre-Roman period: 'already and especially at river crossings, like Beauvais, Amiens, Soissons, and Cambrai, the Gauls had established their capitals. By adopting them as relay posts and garrisons, the Romans infused a new life into them' (Demangeon, 1948, 463). From the La Tène period there is proof that, in contact with the Mediterranean, cities of the Rhône—Saône axis were already active ports: stimulated by Greek merchants, Mâcon and Digoin participated in exchanges bound for oceanic shores and the great tin route via navigation on the Loire, as did Vienne, or relay centres on the intervening plateaux, like Sainte-Colombe.

The same was true in many other parts of the territory: Le Mans, Rennes, Poitiers, Orléans, Tours, the ancestor of Toulouse, 10 kilometres south of the present metropolis. Aix-en-Provence, Nîmes, all these and others had Gallic ancestors and we can marvel at the persistence throughout the ages of the sites of several of our large cities, proof of their good qualities as much as of the foreknowledge of those who chose them. Lutetia, capital of the Celtic tribe of the Parisii, already existed as a small village on the Ile de la Cité when Julius Caesar made his famous Gallic campaign, since he reports that he saw it burning. Chosen by the Romans as a settlement and a crossing, served by the navigable Seine valley as well as by the great *via* (road) which united northern Gaul with the Loire region, endowed under the Roman empire with numerous official buildings (arenas, public baths whose traces can still be found), Paris was to become little by little the capital of the Frankish kingdom, a role established by the benevolence and the monumental undertakings of the Capetians (Notre Dame, the first Louvre, the first fortifications of stone constructed outside the Ile de la Cité under Philippe Auguste in the twelfth century).

The success of Paris in Gallo-Roman times is only one example among many others of the great blossoming of cities which characterizes this period. In the privileged environment of the *pax romana*, numerous important Gallic villages were organized and developed; other towns were created from nothing: Narbonne was the first, then others multiplied along the Rhône and along the southern coasts (Arles, Aix, Fréjus, Orange, Béziers, Lyons, etc.); in strategic places where camps were set up (Strasbourg); at particularly important valley crossings (Rouen, Bordeaux, Nantes, Orléans, etc.); in the centre of basins as markets (Autun, Feurs). Certain typical names have prolonged the memory of this origin up till this day: Fréjus, Feurs, containing the term *forum*, just as Fourvière, *Forum Vetus*, the cradle of Lyons, perched on a hill with steep slopes overlooking the right bank of the Saône, near its confluence with the Rhône.

The formation of this urban network, particularly complete in the southeast, proved to be of capital importance for the future. Remarkable situations at major crossroads, exceptional sites endowed with an environment able to adapt to growth and technical progress, the cities of the Gallo-Roman period continue to play a first-order role in contemporary France: all the largest French cities are 2000 years old: 'of the 44 stations on Peutinger's map, which appear as the chief-towns of the *civitates* [administrative subdivisions of the time], 26 are today Prefectures [departmental administrative capitals], 7 are sub-Prefectures [under-departmental subdivisions], and only 6 are large villages or simple villages' (Lavedan, 1960, 236; Pinchemal, 1969, 380).

The first urban developments

From the decline of Roman power, during all of the Low Empire and a part of the Middle Ages, urbanization takes on another character. The towns no longer develop freely; they are protected by stone ramparts, often made from fragments of monuments built during their time of glory; some vegetate or suffer; others come under the protection of a seignioral sovereignty, capable of furnishing aid and protection. Moreover, the development of the surrounding lands, often by clearing the forest and opening up roads, which facilitate the gathering and commercialization of surplus agricultural products, begins to appear and it enables the towns to be integrated into a nascent system where the monetary economy introduces new forms of relations. Little by little bourgeois urban communities were formed, in some cases strong enough to obtain from the lord, whether he was nearby or far away, lay or religious, charters of freedom which affirm urban independence in the heart of the provinces.

We could cite numerous names which still appear on our maps today. A few economic factors were important, but they appear very secondary during this time, compared with military and religious preoccupations. Just the same we can mention a few crossroads, a few markets, a few places privileged by the use of rivers as an energy source (Mulhouse), or by an ease of transportation (Lille, whose name conserves its original image of a community, situated on an island formed by a real chalk bridge among the network of marshy channels of the Deule).

The château towns guarding river crossings, the well-situated confluences, the ridges between the plains, sometimes had very revealing names: Châteauroux, Chatellerault, Château-Thierry, Châteaudun, Châteaubriand, Séverac-le-Château, Fontenay-le-Comte, Bar-le-Duc, but many other names are less revealing: Amboise, Chinon, Epinal, Sancerre, etc. As the protector, the fortified château still dominates the town, either from a height (Epinal, Bar-le-Duc), or by occupying the culminating point on a hill whose slopes are covered with ordinary houses (Séverac-le-Château), or even simply by its majesty in the midst of the other buildings which are found on the same level (Sancerre). Rivers and châteaux are often associated, and the old city is arranged with respect to the bridge and the donjon in small, cramped, narrow, winding streets. From the associations between an easily fortified site and a favourable crossing point, the middle-sized cities arose when a market was created; the often poorly accessible old quarters are in contrast with the posterior development which was more aerated and grew in the plain or along the neighbouring valley.

The cities associated with abbeys or monasteries, whose founders had often sought an area propitious to calm and to prayer, favoured the development of certain lands, but not the growth of active urban centres. Now like Cluny, Moissac, Saint-Omer, they are small centres, crouched around the original magnificent buildings, often transformed, completed or mutilated in the course of the centuries; the original town centre remains either in the middle of the present-day town, as in Charlieu, Aurillac, Figeac, Brive (where seven thoroughfares converge toward the monument), or on one side as in Cluny. They still remain, if not a spiritual influence, at least an important tourist attraction. Others like Saint-Denis near Paris, Saint-Martial of Limoges, Saint-Martin of Tours, have been swallowed up by the neighbouring large city, where they are only one activity among others. By themselves, these religious foundations have never proved to be capable of stimulating a major urban expansion.

However, from this period on a somewhat planned urbanization existed, and new cities burgeoned. They were the achievement of feudal lords wishing to increase the population of their lands and their incomes, or else tackling the occupation of the provinces and desirous to strongly impose their control. The great rivalries between the Count of Toulouse and the King of France in the thirteenth century, between the King of France and the King of England during the Hundred Years War, the face-to-face positions of the French Kingdom and the Empire, on opposite banks of the Rhône valley ... have had as an effect numerous creations of this type in southern France. This is the period of the famous *bastides* (new fortified towns), particularly numerous in the southwest. Here again the toponymy is revealing: Villefranche-sur-Saône, Villefranche-de-Rouergue, Villeneuve-le-Roi, Villeneuve-sur-Lot, Villeneuve-lès-Avignon. The cities can also carry the name of their founder (Libourne), that of their illustrious foreign 'godmothers': Valence, Boulogne (Bologne), etc. From the twelfth century, with Montauban (1144) among others, but especially between 1250 and 1350, this new form of city develops. One of the best examples is Aigues-Mortes, founded in 1246 by Saint-Louis: its square ramparts ensure protection, not only against the enemy, but also against the violent winds of the Lower-Rhône; on the inside, no street is straight, and the public square is carefully protected against the great north—south blowing of the *mistral*. Aigues-Mortes, surrounded by new exterior quarters, still exists as it was originally constructed.

If the truth must be told, the founders of medieval cities proved not to have had the same touch for choosing sites as did their Gallic or Roman predecessors. Few of their creations rose to the ranks of the great. The most successful are Montauban, Carcassonne, Libourne, and they are by far overshadowed by earlier and later towns. Undoubtedly, as some authors have suggested, we should interpret this as the result of a troubled, chaotic period, where political fragmentation and webs of rivalries determined the choices, based more upon military and religious considerations than upon economic needs or objectives, as was the case during the period of Roman administration, powerfully established in Gaul, in the shelter of the fortified boundary of the Roman Empire (*limes*), or later, in the heart of a kingdom that the monarchy knew how to bring together and enlarge, while at the same time maintaining an increasingly efficient and centralized organization.

'Modern Times'

The period of Modern Times opens up a new phase or urbanization. Henceforth, what might be called the 'network of normal service' is set up: no province was without its capital, no roads were without relay stations related to the types of transportation, no rivers were without ports, no countryside was without its rural market, the habitual site of fairs and exchanges. From now on, the creation of urban centres will be linked with very specific needs.

At the top of the list, once again, the necessities of defence play an ever important role, but the general conditions have changed. The boundaries of the kingdom are enlarged, and it is at the periphery that the new urban settlements increase, integrated little by little into the territory, as the conquests develop. Even the conceptions of strategy and defence change. The fortified château, dominating the city which

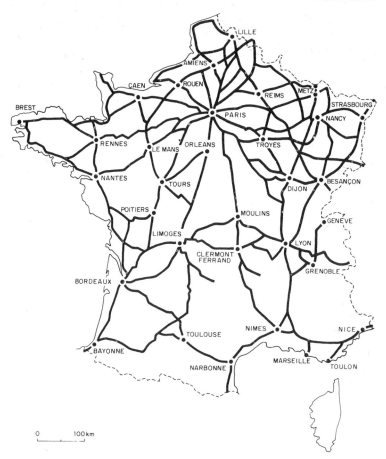

Fig. 8   Post roads at the end of the eighteenth century (cf. Fig. 3, p. 23)

clung to its feet, and serving as a refuge for the city's inhabitants in case of threat, was replaced by the fortified city which was completely surrounded by ramparts, at first classic, then later defensive stonework, star-shaped *à la* Vauban. Numerous traces of these fortified towns are visible on today's landscape: geometric ground plans, like that of Vitry-le-François (1545); concentric-radial layouts where all the principal streets radiate from a monumental central square and lead to a gate in the ramparts (city wall), as in Villefranche-sur-Meuse; fortifications used as decorative areas (Woods of the Madeleine around the former citadel of Lille, the fortified city of Bergues, isolated in its girth of regular ramparts in the midst of the Flemish plain); and numerous cities situated near present-day borders, which have generally grown into large modern cities. Neuf-Brisach (1698) is perhaps the most synthetic example: the outline is a perfect hexagon; the inside is divided into rectangular *îlots* (small blocks), while in the centre is a square, to which one has access from the angles and the middle of the sides; the girth of ramparts and three of the city gates have been perfectly conserved; the fourth gate was destroyed during the German occupation in the Second World War.

During the same period, the expansion of maritime navigation and the discovery of America, draw attention to the Atlantic coast and the creations of new cities followed one after another: Francis I led the way by creating Le Havre at the beginning of the sixteenth century. He was followed by Colbert, who was responsible for the construction of Rochefort (1657), the development of Brest (which was also fortified by Vauban since the enemy could approach from the sea), the construction of Lorient. The economic activity on land favoured the extension of already existing cities (Lyons, for example, went from 70 000 inhabitants in 1697 to 115 000 in 1762; Marseilles from 65 000 in 1660 to 106 000 in 1790; Bordeaux from 43 000 to 109 000 in the same period of time) rather than the growth of new cities. In addition to the ports, Colbert also tried to establish factory towns stimulated by the Royal Factories. However, Villeneuvette, assigned to cloth production (Hérault), and La Glacerie (near Cherbourg) chosen for glass manufacturing, both met with only mediocre success.

Finally, some important people were also attracted by the vocation of town planner. Duke Charles de Gonzague founded Charleville in 1608; Richelieu, in the shadow of his château, established a city (1635). Even the most illustrious personages, namely the great monarchs, shared this preoccupation. Louis XIV, in order to escape the grasp of Paris, established his residence in Versailles (1671) where, alongside a majestic palace, lies a widely spread-out city, whose wisely designed and amply proportioned avenues, converging in an enormous square in front of the royal residence, open the way to Paris. A century and a half later, Napoleon, for administrative reasons, twice revived this gesture by founding cities with a severe orthogonal geometry: Pontivy (Napoléonville), destined to be a military centre, and La Roche-sur-Yon (Napoléon-Vendée, 1804), which has conserved the regularity of its checker-board layout.

Thus ends what we could call the 'classic stages of French urbanization'.

The new urban cycle

Events of a totally unknown nature — a true upheaval of economic conditions — were needed to provoke *a new urban cycle*: the first industrial revolution and the advent of railroads are responsible for this second stage which, perceptible from the dawn of the nineteenth century, was to last in France up until the eve of the Second World War.

The great generator of this first industrial revolution, coal, requires for its exploitation that concentrations of labour are spread out and diffused over the entire extent of the basin. Difficult to handle, heavy and cumbersome to transport by land, it was necessary for consuming industries to be located either at the extraction site or nearby. Thus 'nebulae', urban clusters in the mining basins, were born: black land-scapes, geometric and yet confused, sad, and poorly equipped with real urban cores. Certainly, in France, a country relatively poor in coal, their area was limited: 120 kilometres from east to west, progressively spread out over an average width of 20 kilometres, in sharp contrast with the luxuriant northern countrysides in the departments of Nord and Pas-de-Calais; a triangle about 40 kilometres on a side, touching the boundary of the Saar in the northern part of Lorraine; a few centres around the Central Massif, the most important of which stretches out in the hollow of Saint-Etienne, the unique truly 'black region' in France, since it is the only place where the coal outcrops and where moreover, the black smoke and soot covers over the black of the earth.

Coming from the neighbouring and more distant countrysides, and eventually in great numbers from foreign countries, the miners, often with large families, agglomerated in the coalfields themselves or immediately around them. The same phenomenon was true of the miners of iron ore, but later and only after 1875, on the deposits largely diffused in northern Lorraine which gave birth to two 'nebulae': one in the basins of Longwy—Briey—Moselle (60 km from north to south, and about 30 km from west to east), and a smaller one southeast of Nancy, prolonged by small mining centres extracting rock salt in the Seille valley.

The creation of isolated industrial cities is rare; nevertheless, we might mention one example, Le Creusot. This French factory town was created at the end of the eighteenth century from a hamlet with 165 inhabitants. It was well situated near the Central canal, permitting iron ore to be brought in from Berry as well as coal from Montceau-les-Mines. After the exhaustion of the thin layer of locally outcropped coal, which had encouraged the first establishment, it was subsequently purchased in 1836 by the Schneider brothers, who built an important metallurgical centre. Urban transportation, business, hospitals, schools and the majority of the dwellings belong to the factory which forms the heart of city-industrial complex with more than 35 000 inhabitants. The city lives on itself, or rather on the factory which is widely spread out and prosperous, well served by railroad lines, ramified by means of complicated financial or administrative agreements with Lorraine, from whence it receives pig iron and steel, with Normandy where it partici-pates in shipbuilding activities, and with several foreign subsidiary companies. The company produces heavy equipment for railroads, as well as agricultural and military needs; Le Creusot has a national role and an international reputation even though, it remains almost isolated in the verdant hollow of Dheune—Bourbince, consecrated to stock-raising, except in the very minor coal basin of Montceau-les-Mines.

Another wave of urban changes was provoked by the revolution in communications. This was symbolized first of all by the development of the railroads, facilitating the movement of people and the collection of merchandise, then by the generalized diffusion of the automobile, and at the same time by the multiplication of means of transmission of all kinds of information. Urban change burgeoned around the large metropolises, notably around Paris, transforming century-old villages into industrial or residential cities, satellites or dormitory towns. Saint-Denis or Asnières, near Paris, increased from 3000 to 100 000 inhabitants in a century and a half; Roubaix and Tourcoing, near Lille, increased at the same rate. In other regions of the territory, along railroad routes and at the junctions of the main lines, as well as at the sites of relay-stations or dispatching centres, new towns grew up, populated by railway employees, bustling about in widely spread-out stations, in a tangle of shiny railroad tracks, separated by blackened engine sheds, low and poorly kept-up constructions, repair shops, and warehouses: Vierzon, Tergnier, Saint-Germain-des-Fossés, La Roche-Migenne, Creil, Trappes, etc.

Finally, the ease of transportation did not merely generate utilitarian travel. Leisure activities also increased; the privileged group of people who could travel or take vacations, became larger and larger and, from the turn of the century, cities, developed by the afflux of tourists or by people taking cures at spas, began to flourish. Some were already fashionable during the Second Empire: Biarritz (launched by Empress Eugenia); Vichy; Aix-les-Bains; and, within reach of Parisians by an excursion train or, later by car: Deauville; Le Tréport; Paris-Plage; while Nice and Chamonix welcomed wealthy foreigners seeking sun or winter sports. However, it was only after 1936 and the legislation concerning paid vacations that tourism and vacations in France took on the form of a massive popular exodus and created problems of accommodation.

Since the end of the Second World War

All these movements were expanded, extended, changed in their conception and in their manifestations by the generalized advent of the reign of the automobile and the rapid rise in the standard of living shortly after the second great international conflict. To this must be added the effects of several extremely powerful factors: a rise in the birthrate, the rural exodus, and the beginning of the neo-technical era.

The neo-technical era, or the second industrial revolution, reached developed countries as a result of the enormous scientific and technical progress motivated by the Second World War. Among its principal manifestations, the modification of energy sources should be emphasized: coal, which is heavy, cumbersome, and restrictive by its location, has been replaced by petroleum, natural gas, electricity, and tomorrow, by atomic energy. Factories are gaining their freedom and the industrial landscape can be clean and 'elegant'. It is no longer necessary to locate industry in relation to coal basins or inexpensive means of bulk transportation, such as maritime and inland waterways; instead, other factors receive primary consideration, namely markets, and consequently urban concentrations, while the application of more rational town and country planning imposes other preoccupations. The result is a special kind of urbanization. New cities crop up in the form of industrial *cités** linked with certain large modern factories, for example around the petroleum refineries, the chemical industries, and the

---

* Industrial housing development (individual houses and apartments).

engineering firms close to the Berre pond, where nearly 100 000 people live; these cities are built to welcome and provide housing, administration and leisure activities for a population employed in neighbouring factories: such is the case for Mourenx which in 1960 was the youngest French city. Created from a small village of 270 inhabitants, it already has nearly a population of 10 000, destined to exploit the natural gas deposits near Lacq and to work in the associated factories (extraction of sulphur, chemical industry, aluminium). Many other names could be cited: working-class towns often doubling the constructions which form the older city, as in the Rhône valley, notably in Bagnols-sur-Cèze, housing the technicians and workers of the atomic plant of Marcoule, or in Lorraine, Saint-Nicholas-en-Forêt, the city of a powerful metallurgical firm Société Lorraine de Lamination Continu — S.O.L.L.A.C. (Continuous Lamination Company of Lorraine).

As for the rise in the birthrate which has been registered in France since 1943 as a result of the new family legislation, it has generated a marked change in the demographic rhythm. It has replaced a stagnant population, which laboriously rose from 40 681 000 inhabitants in 1901 to 41 507 000 inhabitants by the eve of the Second World War, with a dynamic population that rose from 40 443 000 inhabitants in 1946 to 52 million in 1974. In the post-war years, France registered an excess of 360 000 births yearly, or in two years a population equal to that of the second largest French city at the time, Lyons. This sudden demographic explosion required a considerable increase in construction, particularly since it followed a long period of torpor, took place in a country whose housing facilities were antiquated, and especially because it combined its effects with those of an increasingly marked acceleration of the rural exodus. There too, France was backward. Before the Second World War, the agricultural population still represented approximately one-third of the working population; it now barely represents 15 per cent; rural youth is leaving the land at a yearly rate of 100 000 to 150 000; a movement which is becoming accentuated, because to a certain extent it is encouraged by the government to facilitate a more rational restructuring of the French economy. A few years ago did not the Mansholt report on agriculture in the six Common Market countries conclude that two out of three farmers must disappear in our country? Without going to these extremes it is obvious that the French countryside had a large relative surplus of population that they are in the process of rapidly losing: in the course of the last 20 years, urban dwellers increased from 21 to more than 30 million.

These two factors led to the staggering growth of our cities. In general, it is no longer a question of the creation of new cities, but of increasingly distant suburban sprawl which has been encouraged by the automobile. With respect to its population, France has the highest percentage of automobiles among the European nations. The dominance of the automobile has had repercussions on urbanization as well as on the increase in commuting over larger and larger distances, and leisure-travel, also encouraged by social progress and the rise in the standard of living. In August, it has been estimated that more than 15 million Frenchmen go on vacation!

Fig. 9   Industrial and urban human settlements

Suburbanization is occurring at a galloping pace, causing both the number and the area of suburbs to increase; cities grow into agglomerations which overlap the traditional administrative limits. Hundreds of resort towns are cropping up along the sea-shore, where they literally hem the best areas, as well as in the mountains, where they sprout up like mushrooms amid fields of snow. More and more urban dwellers own two or even three residences, and one begins to wonder where this wave of urbanization will end.

This explosion of the urban population creates situations which were previously unknown. Indeed, in the second half of the nineteenth century, the number of urban dwellers had increased to approximately 6 million, or 14 per cent when empiricism and *laissez-faire* were the only methods. No pre-established plan had been elaborated; there was little concern for hygiene or attractiveness. We constructed as we could. Theoretically, this is no longer true, and the physiognomy of recent urbanization is profoundly different from that of the last century, and even from the period between the two world wars. Times have changed, in city life just as in rural life.

6
The face of the city

Created for diverse reasons, sometimes transformed during the course of a long period of history. French cities present multiple aspects of an infinitely varied face. Some have completed the full cycle, and walking through their different quarters, we can retrace the periods of vicissitudes which have marked their development. Other cities emerged suddenly, during more or less recent periods, and old quarters are non-existent. Still others, for a long time dormant, have been suddenly awakened by new economic conditions, and juxtapose, not without a certain discordance, the old nucleus and ultramodern buildings. In any case, the exploration of French cities is by no means monotonous.

Sites and old urban nuclei

In this country with varied physical conditions, the first source of variety often comes from the regional or even local setting. Few urban sites are banal or without character: the valleys and the coasts have furnished the majority of general themes utilized. An indentation, a river bend, a confluence, an island, a ford, and later a bridge, a raised bank, a group of hills — all of these were potential settlement sites. In this instance, the plains have played a major role. According to the statistical studies made by Philippe Pinchemel (Carrière, 1963) based on the 1954 census, only one French city of more than 100 000 inhabitants (Saint-Etienne, a coal centre) and only three cities of more than 20 000 inhabitants (Aurillac, Le Puy, and Rodez, three centres of inter-montane basins) are located above an altitude of 500 metres. All four are in the Central Massif, a compact mountainous mass which occupies the entire heart of the country. On the contrary, the Alps, much more deeply carved out and open, especially in the north, offer lower sites, and the Alpine capital of Grenoble is located at an altitude of only 214 metres; it is the southern Alps which contain the city with the highest elevation in France, but it is a small city, Briançon (11 000 inhabitants, 1250 metres); it is followed by Pontarlier in the eastern Jura (16 000 inhabitants, 837 metres). This low altitude is especially noticeable for the large cities, since 85 per cent of the urban places with more than 200 000 inhabitants and 37.5 per cent of those which reach between 100 000 and 200 000 are found in the regions located at less than 100 metres, which occupy one-quarter of the territory.

Nearly two-thirds of the French cities are situated on watercourses and, for the places of more than 20 000 inhabitants, the proportion reaches 95 per cent. Indeed, water attracts men: it is a means of transportation or an opening for traffic; it provides favourable sites for trade; it furnishes an element necessary for life, and many activities; finally it is a source of aeration, of space: cities without water are colourless and incomplete.

Various circumstances can be favourable: an island, as Lutèce (Paris), Amiens; the head of an estuary as Rouen, Nantes, Bordeaux; an easy crossing due to the presence of an ancient ford (Angers, Orléans, Montereau, Brive, Lille, Le Mans); the convergence of waterways, as in Grenoble, Lyons, Metz, Le Mans, Rennes. All these sites incited the first inhabitants to emphasize the river; it is the vital artery of the city, sometimes navigable, always fordable. The first quarters of such cities developed in relation to the ford, to a narrowing in the river or to an island, then in relation to the bridge constructed from this favourable element, and in the direction of which the roads converged. The principal nucleus is on one of the two banks, generally the highest, sheltered from floods; on the other bank, a bridge-head or a small twin city marks the end of the crossing. It is an absolutely typical situation; dozens of examples could be cited; at random, we can mention the following: Toulouse, Orléans, all the cities of the Loire, Angoulème, Le Mans, Strasbourg, Avignon and Villeneuve-lès-Avignon, Valence, and all the places in the Rhône valley where names from the Midi resound and where, for a long time, the Kingdom of France and the Empire occupied opposing positions on the two banks: Tain and Tournon, Andance and Andancette, Viviers and Donzère.

Another sought-after site has been the valley dominated by a hill or cutting through a secondary mountain chain, winding in meanders and leaving only a narrow strip of land easy to defend. Such a valley associates water and natural defence — the navigation or commercial route following the valley, and the fortress protecting the crossing. Le Mans is a striking example of a lowland area; its hill is crowned by a château and old quarters which overlook the bridge on the Sarthe and the opening that results from the confluence with the Huisne. Lyons orginated on the famous hill of Fourvière, perched above the confluence of the Rhône and the Saône, rivers on which it took more than ten centuries to build bridges. Besançon, in the bend of the Doubs river, was for a long time an important fortress; the cluses* of Pontarlier and Bellegarde, the narrowings of Sisteron and Digne, the high basins of Briançon and Embrun, inevitable passage points across vigorous mountain chains, have all been fortified and are still surrounded by the high defensive walls and the strongholds which have protected them for centuries. The inhabitants grouped together on the flanks of the defended hilltops or at their feet; they were connected with the protective elements by rough footpaths, underground passages and sometimes thick high defensive walls.

---

* Cluse: a narrow gorge or transverse valley cut through a mountain ridge; the term is used chiefly of the Jura mountains.

The common characteristics of all these old quarters are: the narrowness of the streets, often rising or circular, or sometimes both at once, following the gradient and the bend of the protective enclosures; the presence of a few old mansions, formerly the residences of wealthy families, now often abandoned to the poorest or to artisans because of their interior courtyards; the sudden appearance on the highest point of the château, which today is often shown to its advantage and visited by tourists, such as the famous châteaux of the Loire valley; the dominating, massive structure of the church, with its more or less streamlined towers, the nave and the chancel supported by buttresses, flying buttresses, radiating chapels, a powerful and at times sumptuous stone architecture which illustrates the faith of the ancients. The great religious edifices, illustrious cathedrals or famous abbeys, have, for centuries, towered above the mass of lower constructions accumulated at their feet, and, even recently, before the last phase of modern urbanization, they alone dominated the constructed area with numerous and slender towers. We think, for example, of the soaring heights of the gothic stone lace of Amiens or Beauvais, the power of the coronation cathedral of Reims, not to mention the regular austerity of Saint-Rémy, the asymmetry of Notre-Dame de Chartres surrounded by a sea of wheat, and the solidity of Notre-Dame de Paris, which rises in the very heart of the capital; the vertiginous verticality of the Strasbourg cathedral, whose pink sandstone glistens in the sunset; the sombre lava decorated with light inlaid stones of the churches in Auvergne: Notre-Dame of Le Puy, Notre-Dame of the Port in Clermont-Ferrand; the astonishing effects of the red brick in the great edifices of the Garonne valley in Toulouse, in Albi; the dazzling whiteness of Saint-Trophyme, of Arles, among the black cypress trees and the Roman monuments. These unbelievable jewels of the old cities and not only the most important ones — how many abbeys or cathedrals, formerly flourishing, are now almost isolated, like Tournus, Brou, Cluny, Saint-Bertrand-de-Comminges, or even in ruins — nevertheless always retain around them a few old houses to which, due to tourism, are added relay stations, well-known hotels or restaurants, illuminations, nocturnal entertainment, etc.

Certain cities have conserved almost perfect vestiges, such as the famous Carcassonne, guardian of the passageway between the two Midis, the oceanic and the Mediterranean, and still surrounded by its double ramparts. It was built on the great Roman road from Italy to Spain: 'From Narbonne to Toulouse stretches out the historic road trampled by the Gauls, the Romans, the Visigoths, the Arabs, the crusaders of Simon de Montfort, the English of the Black Prince, the English in 1814' (de la Blache, 1903). Carcassonne was a fortress on this 'People's Road'. The early centre was constructed on the summit of a high hill, formerly the site of a Gallic fortress, a resting-place on the Roman road; it became in the Middle Ages a fortified centre surrounded by a double girdle of towers and ramparts, inside which the narrow streets crowd around the Saint-Nazaire cathedral. In the thirteenth century a lower city was founded at the foot of the hill: a sort of blockhouse, it has a regular, quadrangular design, with streets intersecting at right angles around a central square shaded by plane-trees; this lower city was also surrounded by ramparts, now destroyed and replaced by avenues lined with trees. The Aude flows between these two cities which are connected to one another by two bridges: the Pont Neuf, modern, and the Vieux Pont, which dates from the thirteenth century, and was built at the same time as the lower city. Another example is the old centre of Poitiers, on a rocky spur, washed by the waters of the Clain: a former Gallic town on the route that links the Loire with the Garonne and which was later utilized by the Roman road; fortified, it became a religious metropolis whence Saint Martin set out to evangelize the Gauls, and its name is famous in the history of the great battles which repeatedly liberated the French territory from invasions: 507 against the Visigoths, 732 against the Arabs, 1356 against the English (Demangeon, 1948, 486—7). On several occasions, a regional capital or even an intermittent residence of the French kings, Poitiers is a veritable museum of Roman art: among its old houses clustered on the rocky spur, amid the medieval calm of its old streets, remarkable edifices come into view at every step: Notre-Dame-la-Grande, Saint Hilaire, Sainte-Radegonde, the baptistery of Saint John, Saint Peter's Cathedral which is built of blocks of chalk marvellously bonded.

The old quarters though marked by common features are, however, often very different, because respectively they attained their maximum development in diverse periods in accordance with the dates of urban prosperity. Bourges, on the road between Burgundy and Aquitaine, has a beautiful Gothic ensemble consisting of its cathedral and the Palace of Jacques Coeur (Minister of Finances of Charles VII) who resided there during part of Charles's reign. Toulouse, 'one of the oldest cities of Gaul' (Demangeon) built on a hill, and then extended downwards onto the right bank of the Garonne, has been, since the first century A.D., a 'warehouse for merchandise, a centre for exchange, the focus of a refined civilization'. In order to protect this rich and densely populated city, it was fortified from the third century, and thus the perimeter of Toulouse was stable up until the middle of the Middle Ages. At that moment, the great prosperity of the 'golden century' which lasted from the end of the fifteenth century to about 1560, caused this too rigid corset to split: the dyer's woad trade enriched the city, which became the great international supplier of this dye, holding first place in Europe. Fifty thousand inhabitants were crowded together there; an active university, a rich middle class endowed it with life; this is the period of the old mansions, which even now are the jewels of the old city, lost in the maze of old, sordid houses.

For many Atlantic cities, it is the trade with the 'Islands', that is to say the Antilles, in the eighteenth century, which enriched them, and it is from this period that date the most beautiful mansions of Nantes or of Bordeaux, the famous 'homes of the privateers' (meticulously reconstructed stone by stone after the fire of 1944) in Saint Malo.

All these ancient developments occurred progressively up until the nineteenth century, and exhibit a clear evolution. In place of frequently rather disordered medieval constructions, a town-planning policy more concerned with balance and aeration gradually took root (Lavedan, 1960). All the efforts of town builders up till the sixteenth century were concentrated on a few seigniorial or religious buildings and neglected even the closest surroundings, but the seventeenth century witnessed the blossoming of vaster preoccupations. Large public squares were laid out, surrounded by monuments and residences that were carefully positioned: in Nancy, the large squares and monumental ensembles by which King Stanislas joined the old and the new city; in Paris, the Place des Vosges, the Place Royale, the mansions which border the Place de la Concorde, on the north; in Toulouse, the Capitol ensemble. Bordeaux is the famous example of this transformation. As Demangeon (1948, 618–25) stated:

> We see this medieval city enshrined among vast and sumptuous quarters which are the work of the eighteenth century, the age of big business and prosperity. Although living off its river, the city up till then had paid no attention to it; only ramparts faced the river. To open the city towards the river, to give the old quarters wide perspectives, such were the concerns of the eighteenth century, of its architects, such as Gabriel, and of its provincial administrators, such as Boucher and Tourny. First of all, the city was fronted on the Garonne by a monumental square. . . . Then towards the Garonne, a second opening was made, the gate and the square of Burgundy, symmetrical to the Royal Square, and between them a quay with monumental façades. Finally the old city was transformed by laying out large avenues or walkways, bordered with houses of a uniform style, along the former moats or inside the central quarters, by creating a magnificent public garden, by erecting monuments such as the Archbishop's Palace (now the Town Hall) and the Great Theatre. It was in the same spirit and to achieve this project that the Restoration demolished the old château Trompette and replaced it with the large esplanade of Quinconces. These extensive public works were financed thanks to the unparalleled prosperity which marked the reign of Louis XVI.

These transformations were evidence of increased security and greater technology, which made it possible to remove the fortifications and often to replace them by large avenues or lanes bordered with trees; likewise, these changes showed that the preoccupations with prestige were no longer uniquely reserved for God and the aristocracy, but wished to reach a new social class, the *bourgeoisie*, whose wealth was by then established. Indeed, all historical texts are explicit; prosperity and town-planning go hand in hand: the former is like a sap which gives vitality to the cities and makes them grow larger and become more beautiful.

In certain cases, fortuitous circumstances promote change. The will of one person can be responsible for the creation of entire cities preconceived and laid out before being built, such as Versailles. Fires destroying the old quarters were frequent in this period and resulted in more or less complete modifications: both Châteaudun and Pontarlier are at the same time victims and beneficiaries; the best example, however, is furnished by Rennes, whose medieval wooden houses with gables and mansard roofs are no longer found except along the banks of the Ille, the fire of 1720 having destroyed almost the entire city, subsequently reconstructed in a rather cold, geometric layout, and thus comprising only a few elements earlier than the eighteenth century (Meynier, 1966, 9–10).

This predominantly empirical evolution continued up until the first third of the nineteenth century. For example, it is sufficient to look at the map of the dates of the creation of streets in Paris (Atlas de Paris, 1967) to see its influence upon certain major roadways and upon some major urbanistic conceptions during the period which goes from the seventeenth to the nineteenth century. Even the housing developments which increase in number, have geometric designs and adequately wide streets. Nearly everywhere, streets and roadways that are too narrow and too winding are widened and straightened; new bridges are constructed; new squares are created, some of which are linked to the transformation of an entire quarter of the city. Such squares, which are often called the 'Royal Square', are famous in Dijon, Lyons, Montpellier and Rennes in honour of Louis XIV; and in Bordeaux, Nancy and Reims in honour of Louis XV. Across the old quarters, new straight streets are laid out, sometimes accompanied by the construction of buildings in a homogeneous style, as in Orléans, Tours, Châlons-sur-Marne; these streets allow one to easily cross the old city and end up at the bridges on the river, the Loire or the Marne. In Marseilles the laying out of a major north–south route, a section of the road from Aix towards Italy, caused an actual break in the old plan of the city; the former ancient and medieval city was deliberately left in the background and the new road became the axis of modern growth.

Everywhere cities begin to stir: only the lack of mass transportation holds back greater expansion.

The revolution of the railroads

This mass of transportation arrives in France after 1837 and the building of the first railroad. By 1860 the railroads are undergoing full-scale development. In 1880 the entire country is covered by a gigantic spider's web of railroad tracks which converge toward Paris; the chief-town of each department becomes a micro-pole in the web through the enterprise of local companies. Henceforth, the urban network has at is disposal a dense concentration of men and wealth, and thus a great potential for expansion. In 1850, one Frenchman out of four lives in the cities; in 1901, two out of five. If we just take Paris as an example, it had 492 000 inhabitants during the time of Louis XIV, 548 000, 120 years later in 1801, in the beginning of the reign of Napoleon I, 1 000 000 in 1851, 3 000 000 in 1911.

Urbanization acquires a new style. The old sites, on hilltops or near bodies of water, were not necessarily adapted to railroad traffic, which requires low gradients and vast areas to construct its infrastructures. The railroad stations are built in the plains, very often fairly distant from the original town centre. The stations were a gathering point and

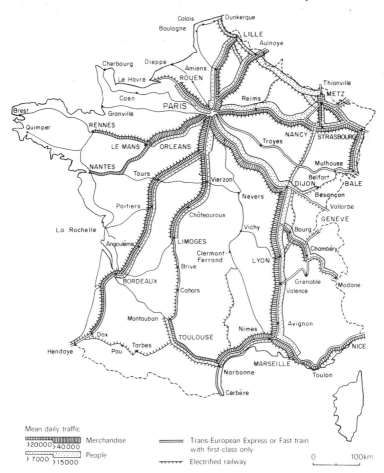

Mean daily traffic

▭▭▭ >20000 >40000	Merchandise	══ Trans-European Express or Fast train with first-class only
▭▭▭ > 7000 >15000	People	┬┬┬ Electrified railway

0   100km

Fig. 10   Main railways and traffic (1973)

the railroad tracks intersected the streets and introduced a linear break in the constructed area. People used to speak of the 'quarters beyond the water'; they will also speak of those 'beyond the tracks'. The railway station is a remarkable point of attraction; always built behind a rather vast square, it is the obligatory terminating point for thousands of 'station' avenues and streets which lead toward it. This square and its avenue are soon the centre of the most active hotels, the most lively cafés, the bus companies with incessant relay and complementary traffic, and then of business which is increasingly varied and multiplying rapidly. A 'station quarter' is created. If the old city was perched on a hilltop, the new quarters move down: thus Laon, located on a butte, which kept watch over the road opening France to the northeast, partly abandons its little triangular plateau, henceforth enveloped in peace and

87

quiet. In Le Mans, the evolution is typical: in contrast with the cathedral and town hall on the hill — the old centre — a new focus of attention arises about 2 kilometres away introduced by the railroad station; between the two are located the prefecture, the large squares for open-air markets and fairs, the nineteenth-century streets with all the departmental administrative services (post office, police station, tribunal, chamber of commerce, etc.); near the station, the grain elevators and the agricultural cooperative of the most powerful departmental association in France, one of the largest bus stations in north-eastern France, and the major hotels developed. Later on, on the other side of the railroad, in the alluvial plain where the waters of the Sarthe and the Huisne come together on the former marshy or wooded lands, large factories manufacturing aircraft, automobiles, agricultural equipment, as well as new residential quarters, have been built about 7 kilometres from the original site, blocked toward the north by hills. Is this still the same city which is spreading out and growing? Where is the real centre? The residents themselves wonder, and the town-planning projects are a challenge with regard to the decisions to be taken and the investments to be made.

But this influence of the railroads is not only directly shown in the general layout of the cities; it brings other modifications to the cities' economy. Cities are no longer essentially markets, centres for trade or craftsmen; many of them become industrial centres or are created to carry out this function: the factory or factories become the principal component of the city. At this time, as there existed no town planning, no legislation about public health or social needs, little urban public transportation, and as the cities were growing very rapidly, the industrial establishments were constructed one after another; the urban land was eaten up with factories; the monotonous geometry of the workshop roofs and brick chimneys is found within a stone's throw of the town hall and the central square. The workers are housed around the factory, under conditions which rapidly become appalling, as the city grows all around and encloses within a shell of stone and brick what was originally tolerable, when greenery and open space were nearby. Thus in Roubaix—Tourcoing, textile factories are found even on the large central square; the streets run between the blackened brick walls of the spinning and weaving mills; in the nineteenth century, housing was constructed to lodge the personnel close to the factory and today these famous *courées* (rows of workers' houses built along narrow yards perpendicular to the regular streets) are being demolished as much as possible: in these narrow and long courtyards the workers lived in frightfully cramped quarters with common pump and toilet and the children played in the gutters of dirty water coming out of the houses.

Mining towns and industrial *cités* were no better off in terms of aesthetics or comfort: the *corons*, originally built to house the miners, stretch out indefinitely, black and symmetrical, monotonous to the point of disgust, with their tiny gardens, their streets all identical, the proximity of sombre pyramids of spoil earth which, in the humid climate of the north, is quickly covered with scarce greenery, the gallows frame of the mine shafts whose sirens regulate the lives of the men, black ants working underground by night as well as day. In certain communes in the department of the North, the Pas-de-Calais, or the northern part of Lorraine, from 60—65 per cent to 80 per cent of the working population is employed by the mine. There is little commercial activity, few extraneous activities; the women who wish to exercise a trade are forced to take buses or trains which bring them to neighbouring towns for the day: for example, in the central part of the North-Pas-de-Calais coal basin, women commute to Lille, where the textile industry welcomes them. Foreigners are numerous in this arduous trade which has little appeal for the French (formerly Poles, now Mediterraneans and North Africans); they group together in neighbourhoods and their families are particularly prolific (Atlas du Nord, 1960).

When these industrial quarters do not completely occupy the city, they are often grouped, more or less close to the centre, in a particular part of the city or its suburbs. They spread out in the low-lying areas where the land is less expensive, the districts situated to the east of urban clusters where the dominant maritime winds pass after having freshened and ventilated the 'wealthy quarters': this is the case in the capital, in Lyons, in Le Mans, and in Caen. The larger, noisier and dirtier the factories are, the farther away they move from the centre of the city: sometimes, similar activities group together in the same district. Thus in Lille, the textile industry is scattered a bit everywhere in the western and south-western parts of the city, the metallurgical industry is in Fives to the southeast. These are now the 'rejected' quarters, dull and sombre. The factories grew there from one day to the next, mingled with warehouses and workers' housing; no monument of value, no thought of preconceived town planning. Little by little, these quarters degenerated and today they are the most sordid areas of the cities, which, if funds are available, endeavour to recover them and transform them. In particular, this is the case in the outer ring of the peripheral Parisian *arrondissements* (municipal subdivisions) — the 13th, the 19th, the 20th — and the adjacent suburban communes which still offer the most distressing spectacle among all the French urban landscapes: the alliance of a rural environment impoverished, out of date, poorly assimilated (small former peasant houses, poorly renovated, former farmyards or gardens full of trash) and of an earlier invasion of urban sprawl, carried out with poor technical and financial means (old workshops or shabby factories, half-ruined buildings, wretched housing), all of which is being abandoned at the present time because no one is interested in this area and only the socially underprivileged live there (foreigners, recent immigrants, the aged, poorly-paid unskilled labourers who are without shelter, etc.).

But during the same period, along the railroad tracks, suburban tentacles begin to grow, in long ribbons where centres form on the sites of the best served suburban stations (Merlin, 1967). The number of housing developments increases: the suburban house, dear to the hearts of the French, with their mean individualism, their little gardens where the family vegetables grow and where a few chickens and rabbits are raised, in short, all an air of make-believe countryside for the rural inhabitants who have just abandoned their village for the enticements of the city. These are the first modern suburbs. Jean Bastie (1964, 116—27) demonstrated how this took place around Paris: the railroads played a fundamental role in the creation of the modern phenomenon of the suburb. Their construction beginning in 1837, later followed by the development of local trains around 1856, trolley cars in 1885, then suburban buses around 1920, was the starting point of the modern transformations of the periphery of Paris, whence about 20 railroad lines radiate. Beginning in 1841 places located 30 kilometres from the centre of the capital (Corbeil) were only one hour away, served by eight trains a day in each direction. The railroad dissociated time—distance from kilometre—distance and democratized travel with frequent and rapid short distance trips.

In a first stage, which lasted almost to the end of the nineteenth century, the convenience provided by the railroads caused an increase in 'lower middle class country dwellings for Sundays, vacations or retirement, which developed in the area surrounding the city and gave rise to the first suburban housing developments'. From the beginning of the twentieth century develops the phenomenon of daily commuting, which enables the activities which are polluting or which require a lot of space as well as the dwellings of the poor, to be shifted to the periphery or outside the city. Thus, in the south of Paris, for example, suburban passenger traffic between 1840 and 1914 caused a doubling in the number of stations, a tenfold increase in the number of trains, while the price of the daily journey diminished by at least three-quarters. Under these conditions, the French capital and the majority of the major cities are witnessing the development of the commuting phenomenon which has been continually increasing since the advent of 'suburbanization'.

The revolution caused by the automobile

But in the midst of this new urbanization as the twentieth century advances a new arrival, the automobile, brings some modifications. While maintaining the preceding trends the automobile gives greater flexibility to transportation: the factory can remain vast and important and be located away from the railroad or the bank of the canal. The city-dweller can live far from his job and, in addition, is no longer restricted by the rigid layout of the railroads. In the suburbs, the ribbonlike pattern of development gives way to a concentric-radial pattern. The intervening empty spaces between the railroads are filled in; in turn, the highways both main and secondary, are lined with a string of housing developments. The most prosperous inhabitants, possessing more than one car, go to live in the wealthy, vast, better ventilated residential suburbs. Even the most modest inhabitants have profited from these advantages, and the phenomenon of the individual house, the suburban house, is rapidly increasing. In the Paris region before 1871, 16 private homes were constructed for every 100 apartments, while this rate rises to 35 between 1871 and 1914, to 87 from 1915 to 1939, to 153 from 1940 to 1954.

Major stopovers along highways develop, just as the railroad centres did, but with different characteristics. Vienne, Villeneuve-lès-Avignon, relays on the road from Paris to the south are noted for their hostelry, their gastronomical restaurants. Marketers of local specialities, like the nougat of Montélimar, are taking advantage of this new fame; repeatedly displayed in numerous shops, in various forms, and advertised on the many billboards along the roads, these specialities become an obsession and almost an obligation for the traveller. Special guidebooks classify the recommended addresses and give the prices at the best tables, at the most well-known hotels, and at fashionable or family resorts; restaurants receive the following mention, enviable among all others, which fairly well defines the point where you have arrived: 'Worth the trip'. Each evening, hundreds of thousands of cars stop; they start off again each morning; in the summer months, highway traffic becomes a veritable nightmare on the main roads.

The population fluctuates: in the course of the day, of the week, of the year, hoards of human beings travel about in gigantic waves, which for the most part take place at the same time and in the same direction. People live on the periphery of large cities, but they work in the centre; they spend weekdays in urban places, but flee towards the country at the least opportunity, in any case for the weekends. Certain quarters are swarming with people on working days and are deserted evenings and holidays, while country houses, abandoned all week, come to life on Saturday and Sunday. As a result, there are inextricable traffic jams, processions of cars at a regular rhythm, a tremendous need for wider and safer roads as well as for superhighways, which although they made their first appearance in the Paris region before 1940, have progressed slowly and are hardly beginning to ease the stranglehold of traffic jams around the major cities. We can speak of a veritable 'road civilization': noisy service stations, motels, and restaurants ('restauroutes') are sprouting like mushrooms along the major traffic axes.

And what is the effect of this revolution inside the cities? For a long time France has resisted: inertia, ill will, and lack of money have combined to paralyse urban changes. It should be pointed out that if we can still move about in Paris in 1975, it is in large part thanks to the premonitory works of Baron Haussmann. If, as early as the Second Empire, Haussmann had not elaborated a plan, well in advance for his time, used not only by himself, but also by his successors up until the beginning of the twentieth century, the French capital would have perished long ago, asphyxiated by herself: his large boulevards and open squares are still the favourite axes of Parisian automobile traffic. But on the whole, French cities are very far behind in terms of the invasion of the automobile which is taking place throughout the country. Until these last few years, the cities hardly dealt with the problem, except by a kind of *laissez-faire* attitude (cars parked absolutely everywhere, occupying almost half the road surface) or by sudden often arbitrary and ineffective regulations (one hour parking zone, parking on one side of the street, one-way streets, etc.). The absence of a preconcerted and deliberated urban policy has been fraught with consequences in this aspect as in others.

The new urbanism

The present-day period marks a change. In view of the demographic pressure and the growing demands of urban life, it was no longer possible to allow anarchy and goodwill alone to preside over the development of the cities. Moreover, the enormous endeavour to be actualized necessitated the use of industrial techniques which were more rapid and less expensive, but generative of uniformity, while the example from across the Atlantic, combined with the high price of well-situated land, encouraged a wave of high-rise buildings.

The change in technology is a decisive element. The Parisian suburbs can, once again, serve as an example: in 1954 they comprise 1 241 000 dwellings, one-third of which are individual houses (three-quarters of them belonging to those that are occupying them). It is this very characteristic landscape that all those who have flown over or driven through the environs of Paris, know well: a myriad of small irregular gardens, in which are arranged, never twice in the same position, never twice with the same design, the suburban houses. The contrast with an English suburb is striking: the one is monotonously geometrical, the other is disordered fancy. The same is true of all the major French cities. And this average taste of the Frenchman has not changed: a survey in 1967 showed that two-thirds cf them have always wanted an individual dwelling. However, statistics, as well as direct observation, show that, since 1955 especially, the huge effort to construct dwellings has been primarily concerned with apartment buildings: between 1958 and 1962, individual houses represented barely 15 per cent of the constructions in the agglomeration. The recent trend is a little different, in accordance with the wishes of the inhabitants.

Here again, let us refer to the work of Jean Bastie. The price of the land is an important factor. Since 1914, the land value in real terms has been multiplied on the average by 50 (Bastie, 1964). The greater the number of storeys, the more the land value is subdivided among the number of participants, which makes for a reasonable incorporation into the overall price of the dwelling. This is a major reason for the construction of apartments over individual houses. Moreover, the industrialization of construction, the technique of prefabricated sections, the use of cranes on rails are much more profitable, and the productivity is considerably increased, provided that we build large units with even façades, that facilitate the mechanization. More important than the architect are the engineer and the financier. Between 1950 and 1960, the production of the French construction industry quadrupled, while the number of workers only increased by 25 per cent; the average size of buildings went from 50 to 300 dwellings. This is a far cry from houses planned at great length and blueprints carefully selected. Procuring a dwelling has become a functional obligation and no longer a carefully pondered choice.

The result is a new landscape characterized by concrete and symmetry, alignments and heights, blocks and towers. They are the apartment complexes (*grands ensembles*) which are multiplying rapidly in France and are the inevitable accompaniment of every city of a certain importance. In 1964 a survey made by I.N.E.D. (National Institute of Demographic Studies) estimated that 200 such complexes, each one containing more than 1000 dwellings, existed in the French territory: 95 of them were located in the Paris region and a little more than 100 were distributed in the rest of the country. Many more have been built since this time. Those in the Paris region are the largest, since they contain more than 197 000 dwellings as opposed to 168 000 for the rest of France, or an average of 2075 dwellings per unit in the Paris region and 1600 in the rest of the country. This type of construction progresses at the rhythm of 60 000 new dwellings per year, and at the present time shelters more than 2 million people: one Frenchman in 25 lives in one of these complexes or 'concentrated worlds' as they have been described by one sociologist. The apartments are modern and well equipped, larger than the average French apartment (3.3 rooms per dwelling); young families with children live in them; they are surrounded by green spaces and parking lots; their building density on the ground is relatively moderate, but they can rise rather high or comprise an alternation of low buildings and high towers, in an often unsuccessful effort to create variety. Among the families surveyed, more than three-quarters feel the advantages of the apartment complex are greater than the disadvantages.

At the time when between 5000 and 25 000 people are suddenly housed in one of these new complexes, it is also essential that they be provided with certain basic services. This has not always been done but it is tending to become obligatory, and the low blocks of schools, the patios that the builders try to make attractive and where the stores of the shopping centre crowd together, now either accompany or are actually located in the high-rise buildings. Often supermarkets or shopping centres take root a short distance away, attracted by an almost assured and well-grouped clientele. But this type of business, which is gaining ground in France, can also choose to locate at a simple intersection of major roads, speculating on the frequency of the traffic: '*Carrefour*' (crossroads) is the name of one supermarket chain which is rapidly expanding at the present time (Chartres, Sainte-Geneviève-des-Bois, Créteil near Paris). These new forms of distribution are also in the process of becoming one of the characteristic traits of the French suburban landscape.

In addition to these groupings, sufficiently large and carefully equipped to claim the name *grands ensembles*, numerous, isolated apartment buildings have been built nearly everywhere. The majority of these recent buildings have one common feature: the number of storeys is above the French average. Sometimes these buildings are incorporated into the old layout of the town, and are close to the centre due to the destruction of old buildings no longer in use; sometimes isolated apartment buildings abruptly rise amid small, neighbouring houses and rival in height the ancient cathedral towers. Against the horizontal skyline of its old Picardy houses, Amiens saw the Perret tower (named by its architect) rise near the railroad station, higher than its cathedral. But generally, unlike cities in America or in 'new' countries like Australia, where the urban core becomes a forest of skyscrapers and

93

where the C.B.D. (Central Business District) is a mass of stone structures progressively lowering toward the peripheral quarters, cities in France have just the reverse structure: the historical centres, up until now at least, are conserved, even protected, as in Paris where in the 'sacred area' (that is, the first six arrondissements which make up old Paris) it is illegal to build higher than about 20 metres so as not to hide the old monuments nor destroy the famous vistas. On the contrary, in the remaining fourteen arrondissements, the height was not restricted and, in fact, increases toward the periphery. Recently, however, it was decided that no more new towers will rise in the sky of the capital.

In certain cities there has been a duplication of the centre: in Rouen the historic quarters of the right bank, where houses of modest height are molded on the concave slope of the meander, around the cathedral, the old market, etc., are now contrasted with the new centre on the alluvial plain, situated on the left bank around the modern town hall: between the two centres lies the Seine and its bridges; the distances are short, nevertheless, a kind of uneasiness seems to weigh upon this distortion of the urban area which is accompanied by a breaking up of the business and cultural centre. The city is no longer a unique centre of convergence, but rather a series of more or less interconnected centres. And one can wonder about the future of these new composite organisms which are in the midst of being created. There are numerous examples of this phenomenon, depending on the former size of the city and its sphere of influence. In Vichy, the most important thermal spa in Europe and the capital of the French spa cities, with a resident population of 35 000 and an additional 100 000 during the summer, there are now three nuclei: the old centre, the parks, and the new part along the banks of the Allier river.

In Nancy, Tours, and Le Mans actual secondary cities have grown up, adjacent to the old centre; in Toulouse new construction has fused from every side but it is still anticipated that, in addition, on the other bank of the Garonne, a new city will be constructed — a twin city, 'Le Mirail', which will lodge 100 000 inhabitants and will provide not only housing but also jobs; the blocks of apartment buildings, arranged in open hexagonal cells like a honeycomb, will break with classical arrangements (see p. 103). It should be added that Toulouse, with 213 000 inhabitants in 1936 and 380 000 in 1968, is one of the major French cities whose growth has been the most rapid in the course of the last 30 years (Pechoux, *et al.*, 1964). However, Toulouse has been surpassed in her speed of growth by Grenoble, the city of the Winter Olympic Games in 1968, which went from 133 000 inhabitants in 1936 to 332 000 in 1968. Only one out of four residents was born in the city. We can treat this Alpine capital, this major industrial city as a 'juxtaposition of cities'; we find a concentric-radial design which is a good illustration of French urban evolution. 'Old Grenoble' is located in the meander of the Isère; the heart is the Grenette Square from where one reaches the 'major centre', a 'bastion of the middle class and business' built between Victor Hugo Square and the railroad station in the second half of the nineteenth and the first 15 years of the twentieth century with well-constructed apartment buildings, avenues bordered with trees, teeming with people and cars; to the north, beyond the railroad, traditional industries and new workshops are located; between the Drac and the Isère, on former military grounds, scientific and university activities, and laboratories, have been pushed to the northwest edge of the city. On the contrary, commercial and banking activities do not go beyond the railroad, nor do the government services which are grouped to the southeast of the old city. But, if up until 1914, Grenoble remained inside her ramparts, the enormous growth recorded since that period has caused the walls to crumble and, after 1945, a veritable exodus has been recorded, especially toward the south (Armand and Marie, 1966).

Likewise in Lyons we are witnessing a veritable upheaval. To the old city on the slopes of the Fourvière hill on the right bank of the Saône, to the traditional quarters which stretch out along the peninsula before the confluence of the two rivers and on the quays of the Rhône which are opposite it, have been added vast, modern industrial complexes requiring large tracts of cheap land and large volume transportation lines; these industrial complexes, with their sprawled-out functional buildings, have invaded the entire lower Rhône valley and the areas in proximity to the railroad tracks in the south-eastern plain, formerly alluvial and poorly exploited. It was necessary to cut into the growing city in order to construct a beltway and major axes of outgoing traffic; and now a 'tower-shaped' administrative centre, the first of this type in France, is being built to the east at more than 5 kilometres from the traditional centre. Supermarkets with their own particular organization are being created from place to place, on the periphery of the town: large horizontal buildings with gaudy advertising, parking lots where cars are lined up, cross-overs allowing access.

Imagination, innovations, everywhere the old structures are breaking up, the look of the cities is changing at a speed unknown till now. The French urban landscapes are gaining in size and cleanliness, but certainly not in variety or in poetry. From one end of the territory to the other, the same geometric blocks dominate the sprawled-out quarters with the same material, the same colour, the same style. We vary the height of the towers, the arrangement of the cubes or parallelepipeds, the size and wealth of open spaces, the name and the advertising of the supermarkets; we construct HLM's (habitations à loyer modéré — dwellings with moderately priced rents) or HBM's (habitations à bon marché — housing with very low cost rents) for the poor; for the middle class and the rich we build luxurious complexes (Parly II, Elysées II) with swimming pools and tennis courts. Seen from the air, what differences are there? Orthogonal geometry triumphs; the curved line appears so rarely that we end up by forgetting that it exists and accustom ourselves to this automatic regularity of the façades.

In the same category with these new urban aspects should be classed the creation of numerous organisms which more or less function as cities, but sometimes with very specialized aspects. Mourenx really answers the definition that we can give to a city since it includes: residence, jobs and equipments according to the principles of the

95

Athens Charter: the tall apartment buildings are separated from the industrial zone by a belt of greenery; the dwellings are arranged in towers in the form of a parallelepiped (2500 dwellings) surrounded by lines of detached houses, providing another 500 individual dwellings. But in spite of undeniable efforts, the dimensions of these new units are too small and the inhabitants feel uprooted (Monty, 1967, 24—6).

In other cases, like Roussillon in the Rhône valley, small industrialized centres have come together and regrouped in order to create a complex unit of 17 000 inhabitants including Roussillon, Le Péage, Saint Maurice and Salaise; three important factories near the railroad (one spinning-mill and two chemical factories) belonging to the Rhône—Poullenc group and created about 40 years ago, have attracted a labour force of which two-thirds migrated from other areas (the majority are mountain dwellers who have come down from the neighbouring Vivarais and a fairly important number are foreigners, especially Spaniards). Around this nucleus of employment, workers' quarters have grown up, at first low and aligned, then, between 1950 and 1956, in apartment buildings two to four storeys high, and finally in scattered and abundant individual houses since 1955. The whole stretches out over more than 8 kilometres. In this disorder Roussillon is endeavouring to constitute a centre equipped with medical, administrative, and social services but the comprehensive plans fail to appear, the community rivalries are bitter and the lack of facilities is flagrant (Rochette, 1964, 173—210).

However, even under apparent architectural order we often find disorder or the absence of a general plan. Many of these building projects have been launched by developers where land was available, but are integrated with difficulty into the adjacent neighbourhoods. Thus it appeared necessary, here also, to put some order into this *laissez-faire* type of development and a plan into the anarchy. In certain respects this policy of urban development can be integrated into the framework of the new formula of which it is an aspect: Town and Country Planning (*Aménagement du Territoire*).

We could sketch the same portrait, on a larger scale for the Montbéliard crossroads where the proliferation of the Peugeot factories at Sochaux—Montbéliard brought about the creation of a cluster of dwellings, a rather disordered and poorly served concentration.

Encouraging the concentration of personnel around major factories, the Parisian headquarters judged it necessary to restrict as much as possible the picking up of workers by bus in the surrounding countryside; nevertheless, workers are still being picked up daily within a radius of 45 to 70 kilometres. That is why *grands ensembles* were built, but haphazardly, where vast tracts of inexpensive land were available, thus apart from existing urban centres, between 4 and 8 kilometres from a central place. These new *cités* are poorly integrated into the neighbouring agglomerations, overwhelmed by this afflux and inadequately prepared to receive it, since they are already very overpopulated. . . . As a result there are profound disturbances in both rural and urban areas. Rural life has been sclerosed by the transformation of entire villages into dormitory-towns, or even sometimes by the coexistence of a *grand ensemble* with an old village drowned in the flood of new houses. Arable lands and meadows have beeñ easily transformed into building sites. . . . The disturbance to urban life has been just as great. Up until now, agglomerations have developed hastily without an overall plan. The collective services have not kept pace with the amount of new constructions. Inter-urban transportation has decreased in quantity and frequency. Industrial monolithism has created a vast, un-organized suburbia, a nebula, rather than a coherent agglomeration (Dezert, 1969, 479–80).

Part Four

Regional Planning

Introduction:
The policy of town and country planning (Aménagement du Territoire)

According to the declaration made by the Prime Minister to the National Assembly on 26 November 1963: 'Town and country planning is a major concern for the whole nation'. And Olivier Guichard, long-time Delegate, then Minister of Town and Country Planning, established the guiding principles which call for consideration of 'the geographical dimension of growth, the underdeveloped areas of the territory, urbanization and rural life, the relationship of Paris with the rest of France'. This policy was advocated in France already in 1950 by Claudius Petit, then Minister of Construction, but it was not systematically applied until after the decree of 30 June 1955 which set up programmes of regional action and divided France into 21 Programme Regions (22 since 1971, when Corsica became a separate economic region). These divisions, for the most part purely economic in nature, were taken into account in planning as of the Fourth Plan. In 1963 the Delegation for Town and Country Planning and Regional Action (D.A.T.A.R. — Délégation à l'Aménagement du Territoire et à l'Action Régionale) was created; then in 1967 a Minister-Delegate was put in charge of the Fourth Plan and Town and Country Planning. Since that time, a specialized Ministry has always existed, either completely independent or linked with another one (Equipment, Interior). Thus the structures which were to lead to a certain number of realizations were progressively set up; these results were often more important in their local or regional impact than in their general conception.

7
Regional planning

Formulated as a voluntary policy to transform the territory and the conditions of regional life of the French people, regional planning has already played an important role in the changes which have been made in the landscape during the last 20 years. Its ambitions are great since it is tackling a variety of problems on a variety of levels: local and limited problems such as construction of a superhighway, decentralization of a large factory, creation of an administrative service in a large city, development of a town plan, etc.; more generalized problems such as the desirable development of an entire natural region (irrigation and change of crops in Languedoc), or of an administrative region (industrialization of Brittany); finally, general perspectives for the organization of the national territory (reduction of the preponderant role of Paris, creation of metropolises to counterbalance the power of Paris — *métropoles d'équilibre*). In the extreme, the purpose would be to establish a planning rigorously orientated towards both the general principles and the details of application for everything that concerns the French territory. In response to the first objective, important decisions have already been made on the national level, such as the policy of industrial decentralization advocated in 1938, but not strictly applied till 1955; in addition, a national, generalized plan, a *Schéma d'Aménagement*, modelled after the Schemas already proposed for several French regions, notably the Paris region, has been elaborated. In order to implement the decisions concerning individual operations, an arsenal of measures have been elaborated (building permits, cash grants for demolition in some cases and for construction in others, fiscal exemptions, government aid, etc.). Naturally, these conceptions and their applications are immediately seen on the landscape, all the more vigorously for having been planned in terms of often new theories or inspirations; they are not moulded into existing frameworks or voids, but rather propose a complete transformation, if not immediately, at least in the long run.

Such action, pursued over the last 20 years or so, has touched numerous areas and it is not possible to make a detailed catalogue. Thus, once again, we have chosen a few characteristic examples.

Town planning

In the face of the anarchy of urban development, several cities have tried to organize their spatial growth by instituting town plans. Among

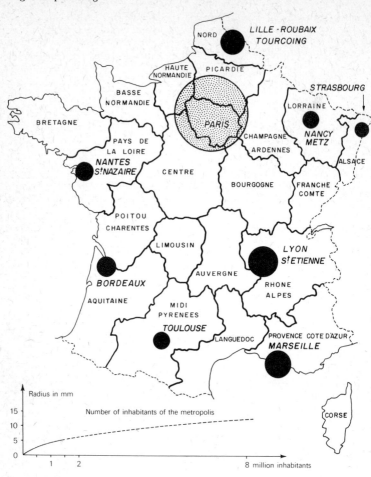

Fig. 11 Economic regions and regional cities which balance the influence of Paris

these Toulouse, with its vigorous growth offers an excellent example: in 1936 the city counted 213 220 inhabitants while the agglomeration counted 365 482 in 1962 and 439 764 in 1968 (Pechoux, *et al.*, 1966, 42–52). The urban structure of Toulouse, in any case, was in need of profound changes: in 1954 the city had 900 kilometres of streets (Paris in the same period had 1100) because a large part of the population, as in many cities in western France, was living in small, individual houses aligned along streets without character; this situation imposed heavy expenses for maintenance of the road system and the urban facilities. Moreover, about one dwelling in ten could be considered a hovel, and 45 per cent had only one or two rooms. After a certain amount of groping a town plan was promulgated in July 1962: aesthetic concerns were mingled with functional, economic, and social preoccupations.

> The residential zone, delimited by the built-up area and by the industrial and university zones, covers 3500 hectares. It is divided into two concentric areas: the first one of which is the 'archaeological centre', the ancient core of the city, and the second, encircles it; ... But while the total population must decrease in the inner area to give way to tertiary activities [*such as commerce, services, transportation, administration ... and everything except agriculture and industry*], it must considerably increase in the outer zone. In any case, the non-polluting industries may remain in these zones. ... The heart of the city is thus progressively stripped of its residential function, and remains only the administrative and business centre. ... The 'industrial zones' are separate (Pechoux, *et al.*, 1966).

The industrial zones are distributed, at a certain distance from the city, in relation to the main means of communication, namely the highways and, for those to the southeast, the railroad and the airport. Already, a portion of the centre has been razed by bulldozers, respecting the monuments and the old mansions, emphasizing and resurfacing some beautiful façades, and replacing the hovels with buildings often occupied by shops, offices, or businesses. All around the centre, groups of medium-sized apartment buildings with 30 to 50 dwellings are sprouting up, in a ring, and even cross the river. Farther on, except to the northwest, the apartment buildings become more and more important; the *grands ensembles* appear, and the heights increase; these are in turn the HLM's (apartments with moderate rents, destined for the low income groups) to the southeast, or others of higher standing; schools, shops, and recreation facilities accompany these new constructions, while vast belts of greenery separate one from the other.

However, on the left bank, a much more imposing project is in preparation: it is the new city of Mirail, which will constitute a kind of 'parallel city', endowed with its own services, but linked with Toulouse for questions of regional administration. The general plan has been organized around wide pedestrian walkways; the buildings delineate a series of Y's, imbricated in various ways; automobile traffic will take place on a lower level; the sinuosity of the streets, the arrangement of the buildings, the presence of squares and covered passageways, the varying heights of construction, aspire to break the impression of monotony which so often characterizes modern cities that have been built all at once. The project covers 680 hectares, 250 of which will remain open space; 100 000 people must be able to live there in a certain number of autonomous neighbourhoods, each having the basic services. As Pechoux, *et al.* (1966) have said: 'The scope of Mirail is unique in France'; but we must add: except for the new towns projected in the Lyons region and in the Paris region (Merlin, 1969; I.A.U.R.P.). One has only to cross the Garonne to move from the city of red brick to the boldest lines of modern concrete. To facilitate traffic through all these new developments, the town plan projects a series of interior roads and boulevards, leading to a parallel external ring-road, already partly completed, which will surround the agglomeration and be connected with the superhighway passing to the east of old Toulouse.

Many other cities have taken stock of their inadequacies and now are organizing their growth through pre-established schemas: 50 years behind, French town planning is now finally making progress.

Overall regional planning

Naturally, in regional planning the kinds of intervention are very varied. It is no longer a question of a punctual or linear intervention, but rather a venture affecting a wide area either directly or by its repercussions. Special groups have been created for this purpose. Some, like the *Compagnie National du Rhône* (the National Rhône Company), a precursor which was created in 1933 and whose efforts have not waned, have been active for more than 30 years. Others came into existence as a result of laws and decrees enacted between 1951 and 1955 in order to rationally orientate a widely distributed regional development programme, since the zones concerned cover, either in whole or in part, 33 departments. There are eight such companies; their locations have been carefully studied to meet the demands of development and to solve specific problems.

The majority of the plains in the Aquitaine basin are divided between two such groups. One is the *Compagnie d'Aménagement des Landes de Gascogne* (Development Company for the Landes (see p. 28) of Gascony) whose task is to regenerate this artificial pine forest, planted at the beginning of the last century, on the longtime unfertile sands of the plains which border the Atlantic coast between the Gironde and the Adour. These vast forests, poorly maintained during the Second World War, have been ravaged by catastrophic fires, while the sale of resin and wood which constituted its main resources, was diminished by the competition of new products. The goal of the company is thus to reduce the risks of fire, put an end to the economic disequilibrium generated by the quasi-monopoly of the land by the forest and attract a denser population by creating agricultural activities: thus the corn fields, the meadows, the fields of asparagus and various other vegetables, are now intermingled with the massive forest cover. The second company, the *Compagnie d'Aménagement des Côteaux de Gascogne* (Development Company for the Hills of Gascony), extends over an area of 1 million hectares, from the Lannemezan plateau to the Garonne and the forest of the Landes; its essential goal is to develop irrigation by actually restructuring the rural economy. Thus, along the small valleys which descend from the centre of the Pyrenees and run down fanwise toward the bend of the Garonne, the irrigation canals carry the water by gravity, pumping stations take the water from the Garonne, small lakes and dams are arranged in the hills, and now the scanty and rare grass, formerly unremunerative, has been replaced by 11 000 hectares of luxuriant cornfields which provide feed for hogs, geese, and turkey cocks; the meadows are richer; the apple and peach orchards climb the hillocks. A company for the development of the *Auvergne—Limousin region* extends its efforts over a large part of the Central Massif; another has as a theme the *development of the waste-lands of the eastern part of the Paris basin*: its jurisdiction extends from the French—German border as far as Champagne, and includes a large part of the Jura and Burgundy. Finally three other companies touch the realm of the Mediterranean: to the east, the *Société du Canal de Provence et d'Aménagement de la Région Provençale* (the Association of the Provence Canal and the Development of the Provençal Region), to the west the *Compagnie Nationale d'Aménagement de la Région du Bas-Rhône—Languedoc* (National Company for the Development of the Lower-Rhône—Languedoc Region), and in Corsica, the *S.O.M.I.V.A.C.* (Société pour la mise en valeur de la Corse — Company for the Development of Corsica).

In these companies, 32 per cent of the capital is furnished by the government, and 68 per cent by local organizations. The results obtained are especially spectacular in the rural domain; moreover, they are strongly supported and controlled by the Ministry of Agriculture. In 10 years of existence they have equipped 100 000 hectares with a modern irrigation system with sprinklers, made possible by the construction of 300 kilometres of canals and 4000 kilometres of underground pipes, eight dams and about 50 lakes; they acquired, transformed and redistributed 45 000 hectares of land, set up 4500 farms; they provide technical assistance for 150 000 hectares cultivated by thousands of farmers; they reforested 15 000 hectares, installed tourist facilities, helped renovate rural dwellings, and even played an indirect but fruitful role in the re-equipping of the commercial networks for agricultural products by the creation of national markets — vast constructions equipped with all the modern improvements, located near the railroad stations, where the products are centralized, selected, packaged, and transported under the best conditions to the consumers — and finally in industrialization (Les grands amen. reg., 1967).

This concerted effort has already obtained appreciable results which are clearly seen on the landscape. We will look at two examples in more detail.

The *Rhône valley* is a marvellous example of a voluntary transformation venture. Penetrating France after having crossed Lake Geneva, where its waters decant and become calmer, the Rhône flows to the Mediterranean across a succession of cluses (narrow gorges perpendicular to the general direction of the folding), of steep rocky trenches that it vigorously cuts down, and finally across alluvial plains where it broadly spreads out. Thus it moves from the cool, humid climates of the regions of contact between the Jura and the Pre-Alps into the sunny lands, warm and thirsting for irrigation, on the fringes of the Mediterranean. It is the most active, the most dynamic of our rivers; the most abundant, since on an average it discharges 1060 m^3/second at Givors and 1669 at Beaucaire (while the Seine only discharges 320 m^3/second in Paris), it is also the most industrious: its waters are heavily charged with sediments (silt, sand, pebbles). Each year it transports more than 3 million tons of material in suspension which encumber its bed and are slowly moved downstream. Floods spread its alluvial deposits broadly on each flank of the river for several hundred metres; the waters stream between banks of pebbles planted with brushwood and carved out by old channels. On the bottom of the bed, sands and gravels move about and eventually settle in a capricious way forming banks which were formerly able to deviate the course of the river. During major floods, the Rhône swept away its banks and overflowed broadly across the whole valley. All its tributaries, except the Saône, locally reinforce its extreme characteristics and each confluence is marked by vast deposition of more or less coarse alluviums.

Across all these recent and coarse deposits, the Rhône flows rapidly: the slope of its bed is steep. It can reach from 0.85 to 2.10 m/km crossing the Jura; at Lyons it is still 0.80 m/km and downstream it remains very irregular: the talweg shows level stretches separated by rapids passing over gorges. It is only in the delta that the Rhône settles down and flows slowly into the Mediterranean between vast banks of sand which are progressively advancing into the sea. During flood periods the speed of the Rhône's waters reaches 4 to 5 m/second, that is to say about 20 km/hour.

These characteristics make the Rhône a beautiful river, difficult to tame: the inhabitants of Lyons waited until the twelfth century to try and build a permanent bridge across it and the construction of this work proved to be replete with difficulties. Likewise, although navigation on the Rhône dates back to early times, and although it knew active periods, travelling upstream always presented serious difficulties. For a long time a system of *équipages* was employed, whereby boats were drawn by 30 to 50 horses. Even 30 years ago a tugboat was able to pull a load ten times heavier downstream than upstream. Certainly, this river did not cross major industrial regions but it nevertheless served the agglomeration of Lyons and, in the nineteenth century, the coal from Saint-Etienne and the wood from Savoy utilized the possibilities of transportation that it offered. It was therefore normal that man should be concerned with its development.

In the nineteenth century the goals of the first overall works which were undertaken were to stabilize the flow by limiting the lateral erosion and the destruction of the banks and to increase the available draft for the boats. A series of diverse works were constructed, according to the technology of the period, along a stretch of nearly 300 kilometres: these works consisted of sunken *épis**, local dikes, destined to stabilize the minor stream and to limit the flood plain. This improvement has succeeded in practically stabilizing the bed without provoking serious changes in the longitudinal profile. However, a more ambitious programme was to be started in the twentieth century. Already the Compagnie P.L.M. (Paris—Lyons—Marseilles Company) had initiated certain works when its task was taken over by the *Société d'Economie Mixte* (see p. 104) created in 1933 under the name of the *Compagnie Nationale du Rhône* (National Rhône Company). This financial body,

---

* A kind of movable jetty made of wood or straw and set in the side of the river to force the water to deposit its sediments.

placed under the aegis of the government, joined together several groups (the communities of the Rhône valley, the National Railroad Company (S.N.C.F.), the National Electric Company) interested in the development of the river from the point where it enters France until it empties into the Mediterranean. The programme established had a triple objective: to better the conditions of navigation; to develop the irrigation potential in the neighbouring plains; to create the necessary infrastructure to produce a considerable quantity of hydroelectric power. To accomplish these aims, the Company envisaged the complete canalization of the Rhône by means of a series of dams transforming the river into a gigantic staircase with 19 steps. In reality, in view of the high population density and the irregular width of the valley, a more flexible programme had to be adopted.

Thus it was decided to construct large dams along the course of the river; at each dam were built a water catchment and a sluice, which rejoins the main course of the river a certain number of kilometres downstream; the sluice, which varies from 5 to 30 kilometres in length, is 170 metres wide, and has an average depth of 12 metres; it is divided into two channels for a portion of its course: one for navigation, and the other to supply a large hydroelectric power plant. The works were begun on the eve of the Second World War by Génissiat, and at the present time they cover the greater part of the middle valley of the river. The major projects carried out are Génissiat (1700 million kWh in an average year) completed after the war; Donzère–Mondragon (2000 million kWh per year, 1952); Montélimar (1700 million kWh in 1957); Baix-le-Logis-Neuf (1200 million kWh in 1960), Beauchastel (1900 million kWh in 1963); Bourg-lès-Valence (at the confluence of the Rhône and the Isère). Moreover, in the immediate vicinity of Lyons, gigantic works have been accomplished at Pierre-Bénite in 1968, at the confluence of the Saône and the Rhône. Finally, other major developments were completed in the succeeding years, notably at Vallabrègues in 1970, at Saint-Vallier in 1971, at the rhythm of one project every 18 months. In a subsequent stage, the Company will be concerned with the improvement of the Rhône valley between the Swiss border and the Lyons region, in the vicinity of the works already completed at Génissiat (Devaux, 1967, 46; Gemaehling and Savey, 1967, 46–65).

On the landscape, the transformations begin to be truly impressive. These works are the fruit of the most advanced technology available in a natural environment that is both imposing and luminous and previously untainted by unclean and out-of-date industrial installations, or even by sprawled out cities. Thus we have the very image of what we might call the beauty of modern industrial civilization: sparkling white building material; a perfect sobriety; buildings with impeccable geometric lines; calm water surfaces, crossing one another and dividing in harmonious curves; modern, powerful factories, sometimes located in the very heart of the mountain or in the midst of orchards and vineyards at the edge of the river. The boldest architectural forms are juxtaposed with old villages with roofs of small, round, faded tiles; the surroundings of the most modern power stations are guarded by the ruins of feudal châteaux, perched on the mountain crests. The alliance

107

between the past and the modern technology of the end of the twentieth century mingled here without the transition of initial stumbling which had occurred at the beginning of the industrial era because of inefficient technology and mediocre resources.

It is necessary to add that the development of the Rhône valley is also stimulated by the presence of two major urban crossroads: the powerful and dynamic Lyons agglomeration, to the north, and the industrial and harbour activities of Marseilles, to the south. In addition, the Rhône valley is the major passageway for all those who are attracted by the enticements of the Mediterranean and, inversely, for the exceptional agricultural products (early fruits and vegetables, flowers, wines, rice, etc.) which flourish in the favourable climatic conditions of the Mediterranean and are then dispatched toward the north to be consumed in the Paris agglomeration, or redistributed in northern and north-western France by commercial organizations in the capital, or even, with the Common Market, increasingly exported to foreign countries. This has encouraged the construction of the first major superhighway, which is now completely finished between Lyons and the Mediterranean, and has been extended south towards Italy, having already reached Paris and Lille in the north: here again, the infrastructures and the majestic layout of the superhighway contribute to the modernity of the landscape. To fly over the Rhône valley, to drive along it, or even to follow the course of its stream by boat, is to discover a new France: well-developed, rationally irrigated or drained agricultural areas; large, modern factories (the industrial suburb of Lyons which stretches out over more than 30 kilometres, beyond the Givors gap, chemical industries, pharmaceutical industries, engineering firms, etc.; large, isolated establishments, like the most important cement factories in France, whose high chimneys cough up a white dust which covers over entire portions of the valley; nuclear power stations and atomic industries); groups of tall buildings in the new towns or in the recent or renovated neighbourhoods of the faubourgs of the old cities; small, individual houses, neat and trim among prosperous fields.

To the west of the Rhône valley, the 'improvement' venture is continued by the *Compagnie Nationale d'Aménagement de la Région du Bas-Rhône—Languedoc* (National Development Company for the Lower-Rhône—Languedoc Region). Created in 1955, the goal of this Company is to reorganize a region which, in 1962, showed by its economic indicators that it was relatively underdeveloped in comparison with the rest of France: agricultural employment still represented 32 per cent of the working population (20 per cent for the French average), while industrial employment represented only 27 per cent (against a French average of 36 per cent). This predominance of agricultural activity was further aggravated by the existence of a viticultural monoculture, dangerous for the regional economic equilibrium, and by a wide dispersion of small farms that were unadapted to technical progress (56 per cent of the farms had an area of less than 5 hectares). Finally, the region as a whole was definitely industrially underdeveloped, and the average income per inhabitant was one-fifth

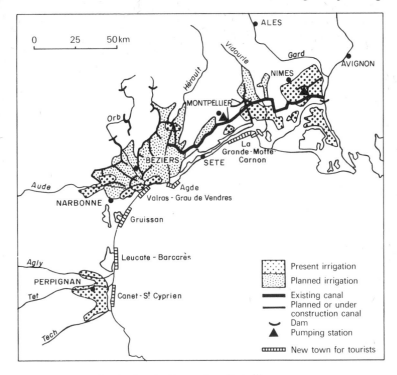

Fig. 12   Future planning for the Languedoc—Roussillon

less than the national average. The projects entrusted to the National Company involve 250 000 hectares, and about 800 000 inhabitants. A work programme was set up in 1951, and first on the agenda was the regulation of water since, as a whole, this region is dependent upon irrigation; water is furnished by the Rhône to the east, and by the short rivers (Hérault, Orb, and Aude) to the west. The first task was to cut a canal 130 kilometres long, fed by the Rhône waters taken out at Beaucaire, and having a discharge by gravity flow of 75 m^3/second, the average summer discharge of the Seine in Paris; this canal is subdivided into several principal branches and is then ramified into a series of small irrigation canals: a third of the canalization and irrigation programme has been completed at the present time. To the west dams constructed at the edge of the mountains bordering the sea will accumulate the waters from the short rivers and redistribute them in the plain.

Besides this new aspect of irrigation, which is bringing greenery and wetness to the heart of the Mediterranean landscape that is generally dry and bare, the most spectacular visible occurrence is undoubtedly the breaking up of the viticultural monopoly: cornfields, luxuriant apple orchards, vegetable fields, and even meadows appear and are increasing. The disappearance of small, unprofitable viticultural exploitations enables regrouping into larger domains; the large arms of

109

the most modern sprinkler systems rotate, dispersing beneficient moisture over wide areas of renewed greenery. To utilize this new production, canning factories have been installed in the region: in Nîmes, in Saint-Gilles-du-Gard, in Vauvert (the latter is a subsidiary of a major American company, LIBBY, and its installation met with a good deal of resistance, but it now strongly helps to orient the local production through very precise purchasing contract); other canning factories are planned; housing is being modernized; the villages are coming to life again; new buildings are constructed; houses are freshly painted; a modern water supply and electrification abolish old drudgeries.

However, the action of the *Compagnie Nationale du Bas-Rhône— Languedoc* is not limited to rural developments: it is also concerned with the littoral which, from Grau-du-Roi to the coast of Roussillon, offers 150 kilometres of sandy beaches, still almost unspoiled. Seven major seaside resorts are being built in this region. And we can estimate that 10 years from now, this coast will be covered by a succession of ultra-modern buildings and developments destined to put the sun and the sea at the disposal, not only of the French, but of all Western Europeans. Afforestation was begun in 1964 to provide a pleasant setting for touristic developments. Already the first resort, the Grande-Motte, has sprung up: here again, an ultramodern landscape is cropping up on the fringe of a territory that until now was almost abandoned (Lamour, 1963, 11—33; Les grands amen. reg., 1967). All along the shores, the other resorts are growing: either small individual houses on wharfs dividing the sea into basins where boats are at anchor or many stores, modern geometric white buildings with apartments for tourists, shops, restaurants and everything for daily life and pleasure.

8
The problem of Paris

The Paris agglomeration occupies an exceptional place in France. At the last census in 1975 the agglomeration had a population of 9 800 000 reaching nearly 10 million: after having sheltered nearly 3 million inhabitants in 1911, the agglomeration's dense core, Paris, now contains 2 300 000 inhabitants within limits that have remained unchanged since 1860; the balance of the population, some 7 500 000 persons, is distributed in peripheral rings of varying densities, which occupy a circle with a radius of about 30 kilometres and are prolonged in more or less distant tentacles along the major highway and railway axes (Atlas de Paris, *passim*; Sch. dir. de la Rég. paris.; Sch. dir. de Paris).

Portrait of the Paris agglomeration

This agglomeration has seen its population increase nearly tenfold since the dawn of the nineteenth century. This growth has created very varied landscapes. Leaving from the Ile de la Cité, cradle of Lutetia, and the banks of the river Seine, one first of all crosses the old, historic centre characterized by serried buildings, four or five storeys high, narrow streets with picturesque names; these are the quarters where the humble folk dwell and the workshops of small craftsmen are crowded together. They are intersected by a few large streets and are embellished with the capital's most beautiful monuments, whose recently cleaned stone sparkles in towers, magnificent façades, and majestic courtyards. Some artists and certain wealthy families are transforming the old apartments into fashionable dwellings. Traffic is intense and very often at a standstill because the tiny streets are unceasingly congested. Centres of night life are multiplying around Saint-Germain-des-Prés, Saint-Séverin, and tomorrow undoubtedly around the renovated quarter of Les Halles. Such is the character of the greatest part of the first six arrondissements in Paris.

To the northeast the 10th and 11th arrondissements consist of mediocre buildings without much character, where crafts, offices, and factories are mingled; the North and East railroad stations occupy large areas; the population is dense and poor; the Saint-Martin canal, a calm waterway abandoned to fishermen, was once doomed to be destroyed and replaced by a superhighway for in-city traffic, but now it has been decided to preserve it as an open-air space. To the northwest, the 9th and especially the 8th, but also the northern part of the 16th and the

111

southern part of the 17th, belong to the central business district: mighty blocks of solid and well-built buildings, essentially from the nineteenth and the beginning of the twentieth century; an accumulation of offices and business, swarming with traffic during workdays, all bears witness to prodigious activity and a great concentration of wealth; the number of inhabitants is tending to decrease, but nocturnal crowds are still attracted to such famous areas as the Champs-Elysées, the Boulevards, the Opera, etc. To the southwest, the 7th is a calm arrondissement, which a part of the 6th resembles: ministries, embassies, convents occupy numerous mansions having their own private gardens; the residences are middle class; commerce and business are subordinate to the residential function. Lastly, to the southeast, a portion of the 5th, actually part of the historic centre, has, in addition, a special trademark because it is the site of numerous university buildings: it is the famous Latin Quarter, the Saint-Geneviève mountain. Here, around the Panthéon, there throngs young people, where all races are mingled, the imbroglio of heteroclite vehicles, the abundance of movie theatres, cafés, restaurants, often exotic, appeal to students and attract by curiosity or fellowship many foreign and French visitors.

All around this central block, corresponding to the first eleven arrondissements, and essentially to Paris before 1860, the peripheral ring of arrondissements is clearly different. Paradoxically, one century later one still feels their late annexation. The administrative divisions of the nine outer arrondissements are much larger. The heterogeneity of the constructions is much more apparent. Alongside still somewhat rustic old houses (Montmartre or the Gobelins area) and the old quarters of detached housing (Auteuil), large apartment buildings of the late nineteenth and early twentieth century, in stone, border the squares and the boulevards; others, in brick, occupy a large part of the extreme outer ring of the city, beyond the outside boulevards, the famous Maréchaux boulevards: these last buildings were constructed around 1930; all around, a ring-road was constructed between 1956 and 1973: a kind of superhighway, partly underground, which encircles the capital. At the present time, these quarters are the theatre of the most important changes. While the height of the buildings is strictly regulated in the centre of Paris (a maximum of eight storeys in the first six arrondissements) so as not to overwhelm the old monuments and destroy the gentle amphitheatre of the natural site, construction in the outer arrondissements was for many years unrestricted and buildings 25 and 30 storeys high have sprouted up here and there; but since 1973, the height is limited in this peripheral ring too. Among the residences, workshops and even factories, occupy vast areas, as do the railway infrastructures. The largest industrial establishments must leave Paris; they are often replaced by apartment buildings surrounded by green areas; *îlots* are regrouped or divided and even someone who knew certain quarters 10 years ago, now has difficulty finding his way.

These outer arrondissements are barely distinguishable from the first ring of suburbs: the landscape is the same in Vincennes as in the 12th, in Montrouge as on the fringes of the 14th. However, a break does exist. It consists of a double ring: the ring-road and the open spaces of the former fortified zone, which for a long time remained an area *non aedificandi* and is now occupied by athletic fields, race tracks, schools. This break is prolonged by two forests, the Bois de Vincennes and the Bois de Boulogne, miraculously preserved since the nineteenth century, and constituting the 'lungs' (large green spaces) of Paris. In the towns contiguous to the capital, the population is very dense; many of them have 100 000 inhabitants, housed in apartment buildings several storeys high, as in Asnières, Saint-Denis, Boulogne, etc. Their territory is saturated, as Paris's is, and their population is tending to decrease. Factories are larger and more numerous, especially in the north, the northeast, and the southeast. On the contrary, the western suburb, which is near the 'wealthy quarters' and the central business district, is more residential, more ventilated, more middle class. The economic and social contrast, which used to be clearly apparent throughout Paris between the more working-class east and the more well-off west, and which is now disappearing owing to the almost uniform high price of new constructions, is also visible in the suburbs by the style of the houses, the size of the gardens, the general atmosphere in the respective areas. Beyond this 'dense ring', is a more ambiguous zone. The urban centres are smaller, the densities lower; one has the impression of truly entering the dormitory-suburb. The working population leaves every morning to go and work in Paris or in the recently implanted industrial zones, which surrounded by lawns and flower-beds, served by parking lots, and presenting an image of industry that one was hardly accustomed to in Western Europe, even 50 years ago. The sea of individual houses is becoming the rule, even if, more and more, it is interrupted by the large apartment buildings of the new *grands ensembles*; rural parcels, truck farms or nurseries, parks, even bits of forest creep in between the built-up areas; along rivers, canals and railroads, the quays, the warehouses, and the factories still outnumber the houses; commercial and military airports occupy vast, denuded areas; everywhere construction sites bear witness to the galloping demographic increase, while parking lots, junkyards, supermarkets, etc., mark the active progress of the urban fringes, not yet saturated, but fed by rapid growth and continuous traffic from Paris toward the rest of the country and vice versa.

The struggle against Paris's excessive power

Thus the great agglomeration little by little creeps into the countryside and the rare internal open areas are progressively swallowed up by urban metamorphosis. Administratively, the frame is made up of the Paris region which, according to the law passed 10 July 1964 and put into effect as of 1966, is subdivided into eight departments: to the east the Seine-et-Marne essentially rural and traditional, to which has been added a department representing the city of Paris alone, and six others resulting from the division of two former departments, the Seine and the Seine-et-Oise: Hauts de Seine, Val-de-Marne, Seine-Saint-Denis, Val-d'Oise, Yvelines, Essonne. Why this subdivision? It is related to the policy of *aménagement du territoire*, which began to preoccupy the

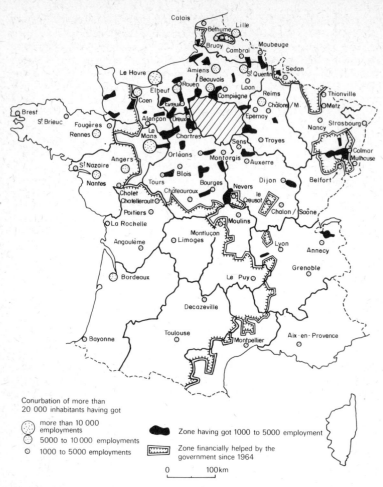

Fig. 13 Industrial decentralization (after Professor Jean Bastie's unpublished work)

government in 1950. Indeed, if, already in 1936, some felt that the weight of the agglomeration was excessive compared with France as a whole, it was only in 1950 that the first serious measures to dismantle the bastion of Parisian power, were launched. Beginning in 1955 major decrees codified the policy of decentralization, first of all by prohibiting the creation of any new industry in the region (7 January 1955), then by advocating the decentralization of government and public services (4 April 1955), finally by prohibiting even already existing factories from enlarging their existing surface area by more than 10 per cent (31 December 1958). To complete the regulation, it was also prohibited to construct office buildings of more than 1000 square metres (5 January 1959) and cash grants were established for the destruction of industrial premises and offices, as well as taxes for the construction of these same establishments (2 August 1960).

The results of this policy are modest but nevertheless significant. Industrial decentralization in particular has given rise to numerous tangible movements: it is estimated that approximately 2000 operations of decentralization took place, that is to say industrial establishments which either left Paris or created provincial branches. This movement involves about 300 000 jobs and taking into account the workers' families it must signify that approximately 1 million people have thus been retained *en province* (all areas outside the Paris region) and did not come to increase the crowd of Parisians. In addition a certain number of activities left Paris proper to locate in the more or less distant suburbs. This is the phenomenon referred to as 'loosening', which at the present time is helping to bring jobs and places of residence closer together in the agglomeration, and to better equilibrate the territory even in the Paris region. Most of the industrial premises thus abandoned have been razed and housing or offices have been constructed in their place: thus the arrondissements in the north-eastern part of Paris are seeing their physiognomy progressively change and the tall residential towers of Belleville, for example, are rising on what a short time ago used to be a centre of crafts and the site of still semi-rural residences. However, it is not desirable that this movement of de-industrialization of the capital be too pronounced, and it is necessary to supervise the operations with great care.

Nevertheless, in spite of these efforts the agglomeration occupies a disproportionate place in the country, in many ways. First of all, the demographic increase has not ceased. Between 1962 and 1968, the population increased by 7.9 per cent: if this progression is inferior to that of all other French agglomerations except Lille (Lyons: +14.8, Marseilles: +14.9, Toulouse: +20.3), it is still too high. But between 1968 and 1975, the rate of growth has been only equal to the general rate for France. Moreover, it should be observed, that the increase is due this time more to the excess of births over deaths than to the influx of provincials or foreigners into the capital. Nevertheless, the proportion of the Paris region's population in France is still very high and reaches 18.6 per cent. There is, in addition, an extraordinary concentration of jobs in the agglomeration. Around 1901 it was estimated that there were about 100 000 commuters living in the suburbs and coming to work in Paris; this number amounted to 448 000 in 1931 and is now close to 1 300 000, increasing at the average rate of 100 000 a year. This is translated by an influx of cars and public transport in the morning and by inextricable traffic jams in the evening, at the time when all the suburbanites leave their jobs. Between 1962 and 1968 the annual daily traffic of private cars at the entrances to Paris increased by 34 per cent and suburban train traffic from certain stations increased by 56 per cent; for example, at Paris/Lyons Station. Thus the excessive concentration of population and activities remains as disquieting as ever.

Paris also has an over-important influence on French life in general. It is not merely an administrative capital, it is a veritable centralist

115

tyrant. No decision can be made on the regional level or even the local level without having been transmitted for discussion and approval by the Parisian central services. This creates a 'red tape paralysis', a considerable delay in decisions, and also causes errors because the central services are not always exactly informed about what is the best, the most effective, or the most economical, 500 or 1000 kilometres away.

To this monopoly of decision, Paris adds a considerable economic and financial pre-eminence: 28 per cent of industrial employment, but more than half the aeronautical, specialized metallurgy, and printing and publishing industries, etc., are concentrated in the Paris region; 40 per cent of the commercial employees, 64 per cent of the head offices, are found in the capital! During the Fifth Plan, 24 per cent of the available funds in France were allotted to the Paris region; for the Sixth Plan, 20 per cent are allotted.

Thus one can speak of a veritable battle, 'Paris versus the Provinces', and if many are denouncing the difficulties or even the scandal, the solution does not appear close, unless the policy of 'regionalization' of the French territory envisaged at the present time is developed in an effective and sincere manner.

The projects for internal restructuring

In addition to these general difficulties requiring solutions on the national level, the need to find solutions for the development of the agglomeration itself should be mentioned. Indeed, even assuming that the growth of Paris is slowing down and will only reach a total of 10.5 to 11 million inhabitants around 1985, it will nevertheless be necessary to house an additional 1 million inhabitants between now and then, that is to say, to construct half a new Paris in less than 10 years. It is in thinking about these perspectives for the future that a team from the *District de la région parisienne* (District of the Paris Region) then under the leadership of Paul Delouvrier, had prepared the *Schéma directeur d'aménagement et d'urbanisme de la région parisienne* (General Guidelines for Development and Urbanism in the Paris Region) published in 1965 and elaborated in 1968 by the *Schéma directeur de Paris* (General Guidelines for Paris), this prepared by the department of urbanism of the capital's Prefecture. What are the measures projected by these two plans to avoid the complete asphyxiation of the agglomeration? The regional guidelines are based on two principles: stop the concentric-radial growth which is threatening to suffocate the centre and replace it by a *linear development* parallel to the major natural axes of the regional landscape. The constructions would be located preferentially on the edges of the plateaux, avoiding intrusion on the valleys of the Seine and the Marne which are to be developed as arteries of communication and protected green areas; the lateral limits of the agglomeration would be marked by the forests of Montmorency to the northwest, Rambouillet to the southwest, Fontainebleau to the southeast, and the new giant airport of Roissy-en-France to the northeast. Inside this zone approximately 80 kilometres long from northwest to southeast, the second principle of the project is to increase the secon-

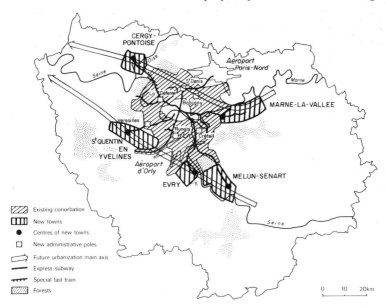

Fig. 14   Future plan for the region of Paris

dary nodes of attraction and to put an end to the strong centripetal force exerted by Paris: this modification would be obtained by creating 'new towns' which would serve populations of from 300 000 to 700 000 and would be complete urban centres, that is to say, not only places of residence, but also places of work and leisure activity for its entire dependent population. The very ambitious initial schema planned eight new towns of this type: Mantes in the Seine valley at the extreme north-western tip; Noisy in the Marne valley at the extreme eastern edge; Cergy-Pontoise, Beauchamps at the foot of the Montmorency forest; in the south two cities on the Trappes plateau; and two others — Evry and Tigery — twin cities on opposite banks of the Seine southeast of the capital. Thus the agglomeration would take on a new appearance. Some of the schema's conceptions have been rather severely criticized, in particular the sites of the new towns, judged by many to be too close to the principal node, Paris.

Where do we stand ten years after the publication of the general guidelines? The new towns, in spite of all opposition, are in full development and already strongly imprint their appearance on the landscape. In the beginning the Real Estate Agency, the District's financial organization, purchased a portion of the necessary land to establish their centres. Teams of architects and town planners began their work and elaborated the basic plan and the developments of most parts of the new quarters. Indeed, the initial project was too ambitious and it would have been too heavy a burden on the national budget. Thus the number of new towns was reduced from eight to five. Being developed

117

at the present time are: Cergy-Pontoise, where the prefecture is in service and the administrative quarter already largely built; Evry, well-served by the south superhighway, a national highway and a railroad, whose construction is very advanced; Trappes, reduced to a single town which will be broken up into a number of quarters more or less engulfed in the greenery and dales of the plateau which slopes toward the valley of Chevreuse; Noisy, the town in the Marne valley, whose linear conception in successive hexagons will permit a wide development and seems to be very appealing. In addition, north of Melun an urbanization project is underway which will extend as far as the edge of the Sénart forest; thus the proposed new town of Tigery will not be built. Some towns have already changed their names: Trappes has become Elancourt-Maurepas and Noisy is Marne-la-Vallée. The other creations envisaged have for the moment been abandoned. To further such restructuring of the agglomeration which must change from stifling monocentrism to more harmonious polycentrism, a whole network of superhighways and rapid mass transit has been planned and has begun to be executed: the Sixth Plan has begun the construction of a large portion of it, and in particular the superhighway and railroad connections of all the new towns with Paris. Some new means of transportation are even to be used, such as the R.E.R (Regional Express Underground). In addition to these new towns some clusters of high-rise buildings have risen more or less planned in the beginning within the agglomeration: such as La Défense, a huge accumulation of high offices towers in the NW, along the extension of the Champs-Elysées beyond the Arc de Triomphe; another one is the town of Créteil which already gathers more than 70 000 inhabitants.

As far as Paris is concerned, the spontaneous renovation is going along at a good pace. In spite of the high price of land, the developers are building rather luxurious apartments (only 10 per cent are low income dwellings) which are rising in tall towers along the banks of the Seine in the 15th arrondissement, in the Italie quarter, in Belleville, and are in the process of progressively transforming the peripheral quarters of the capital. In addition, entire sections are undergoing planned renovation. At the end of all these operations the French capital will have a new face, and it is hoped to maintain a population of about 2 400 000 inhabitants. But, contrary to the present appearance, only the historic core will be preserved with relatively low buildings in the heart of which the great monumental perspectives will stand out; in the peripheral arrondissements where the height of the constructions has not always been restricted, skyscrapers are already rising, like the famous Maine-Montparnasse tower which, with the spire of the Eiffel Tower, dominates the Paris skyline. This ancient 2000 year-old capital is thus undergoing major transformations: already, it is difficult to recognize certain old quarters and we can say that in 20 years, except in the first six arrondissements, the physiognomy of Paris will have almost completely changed. Every year an area as large as the actual town of Paris is to be added to the agglomeration in order to be able to build all the necessary buildings!

Conclusion

A diverse and dynamic France

Throughout the brief and different chapters of this book the image that deserves to be retained, is that of a country where one cannot travel 100 kilometres at a stretch without coming upon a change in the landscape.

France was already the country with three kinds of relief arranged in various ways, of three zones of climatic influence with a changing balance, of millenia of prehistory and history, of peoples come from all corners of the horizon, superposed and mingled. She is today the country of the past and of the future; charged with history, heavy with an aging population, she nevertheless rebounds with the afflux of impatient youth. Propitious to agriculture which was her source of wealth, she now turns with ambition and method toward increased industrialization. For a long time predominantly rural, she sees her children accumulate in increasingly large, modern, bustling cities. From all this, it is the variety of the landscapes which proves to the geographer, the traveller, and the tourist, that they are crossing a small territory, certainly, weighed down by its past, but which feels full of promise for tomorrow.

References

(* indicates titles recommended for further reading)

Abrard, R. (1948) *Geologie de la France*, Paris.

Allen, K. and Maclennan, M. C. (1970) *Regional Problems and Policies in Italy and France*, London.

Armand, G. and Marie, C. (1966) *Grenoble: Notes et études documentaires*, No. 3288, La Documentation Française, Paris.

Armengand, A. (1968) *La population française*, Paris.

Atlas de la France rurale (1968), Paris (published under the direction of J. Duplex), cahier de la Fondation des sciences politiques.

Atlas de l'industrie française (1959) Paris.

Atlas de Paris et de la Région Parisienne (1967) Plates 31.1, 31.2 and the commentary by R. Roulean, pp. 57—72 and *passim*.

Atlas du Nord (1960) (*passim*: maps and commentaries), Paris.

Atlas industriel de la France (1959) Paris (published under the direction of R. Giry).

*Bastie, Jean (1964) *La croissance de la banlieue parisienne*, Paris.

Beaujeu-Garnier, J. (1954) 'Essai de morphologie limousine', *Revue de géographie alpine*, vol. xlii, 269.

* Beaujeu-Garnier, J. (1970) *La population française*, 2nd edn, Paris.

* Beaujeu-Garnier, J. (1973) *Le relief de la France*, Paris.

Bertrand, L. (1944—46) *Histoire Géologique du sol français*, 2 vol., Paris.

Blanchard, R. (1956) *Les Alpes occidentales*, vol. 7, Essai d'une synthèse.

*Bloch, Marc (1951) *Les caracteres originaux de l'histoire rurale française*, Belles Lettres, Paris.

Bomer, B. (1954) 'Le relief du Limousin septentrional', *Mémoires et documents du CNRS*, vol. 4, p. 165.

Brunet, Pierre (1960) *Structure agraire et économie rurale des plateaux tertiaires entre la Seine et l'Oise*, Caen.

Carrière, F. and Pinchemel, Ph. (1963) *Le fait urbain en France*, Paris.

*Chabot, G. (1969) *Géographie Regionale de la France*, 2nd edn, Paris.

Champier, L. (1956) 'Une série de notes et comptes-rendus sur "Les terroirs"', *Revue de Géographie de Lyon*, No. 2.

Cholley, A. (1960) Remarques sur la structure et l'évolution morphologique du Bassin Parisien, AGF No. 288—9, pp. 2—25.

Cholley, A., *et al.* (1956) 'Carte morphologique du Bassin de Paris', *Mémoires et documents du CNRS*, vol. 5.

Damette, F. (1968) *Le territoire français et son aménagement*, Paris.

Dechelette, J. (1928) *Manuel d'archéologie prehistorique et Celtique*, Paris.

Demangeon, A. (1910) 'Le relief du Limousin', *Annales de géographie*, p. 20.

*Demangeon, A. (1946 and 1948) 'France économique et humaine' in *Géographie Universelle*, 2 vol., Paris.

Dermigny, L. and Brunet, R. (1967) Chapters X and XII in *Histoire du Languedoc*, Toulouse (published under the direction of Philippe Wolf).

Derruau, Max (1949) *La grande Limagne auvergnate et bourbonnaise*, Clermont-Ferrand.

Devaux, P. (1967) *Les récents travaux de la Compagnie Nationale du Rhône*, Cahiers Français. Edition de la documentation française, No. 120.

*Dezert, Bernard (1969) *La croissance urbaine et industrielle de la porte d'Alsace*, Paris.

*Dion, Roger (1934) *Essai sur la formation du paysage rural française*, Tours.

*Dion, Roger (1946) 'La part de la géographie et celle l'histoire dans l'explication de l'habitat rural du Basin Parisien', *Bull. Soc. Géogr. de Lille*.

*Dion, R. (1959) in *Histoire de la vigne et du vin en France, des origines au XIXème Siècle*, Paris.

Dion, Roger (1961) 'Le "bon" et "bean" pays nomme Champagne pouilleuse', *Information géographique*, No. 5, p. 209.

Duby, G. (1962) *L'économie rurale et la vie de campagnes dans l'occident médieval: France, Angleterre, Empire, IX:XV siècles*, Paris.

Duby, G. (1970) *Histoire de la France*; vol. 1, *Naissance d'une Nation*, Paris (several contributors).

Duby, G. and Mandron, R. (1964) *A History of French civilization*, trans. Blakely Atkinson, New York.

Dugrand, Raymond (1964) *La garrigue montpelliéraine*. Thèse, Paris.

Dumont, R. (1956) *Voyage en France d'un agronome*, 2nd edn, Paris.

Duval, P. M. (1953) *La vie quotidienne en Gaule Romaine pendant la paix Romaine*, Paris.

East, G. (1962) *An Historical Geography of Europe*, 4th edn, London.

Espace economique française — Etudes et conjuntures. Fasc. I, 1965.

Faucher, D. (1945) 'Evolution des types de maisons rurales', *Annales de Géographie*.

Faucher, D. (1949) *Géographie agraire*, Toulouse.

Fauchon, J. (1954) *Economie de l'agriculture française*, Paris.

Fromont, P. (1962) *Problèmes d'économie rurale*, Paris.

Gemaehling, G. and Savey, P. (1967) 'Un exemple d'aménagement à buts multiples: le Rhône', in *Les grands aménagements régionaux*.

Gignoux, M. (1960) *Géologie Stratigraphique*, 5th edn, Paris, p. 504.

Gognel, J. (1948) *Géologie de la France*, Paris.

Guichard, O. (1965) *Aménager la France*, Paris.

Guilcher, A. (1948) 'Le relief de la Bretagne meridionale'. Thèse, La Roche-sur-Yon.

I.A.U.R.P. (Institut d'Aménagement et d'Urbanisme de la Région Parisienne): numerous articles in 'Les Cahiers de l'I.A.U.R.P.

Joris, A. (1970) 'L'essor du XII siècle', in Duby, G., *Histoire de France*, ch. 10, 3 vols, Larousse, Paris.

Juillan, C. (1903) *La Gaule romaine.*

*****Juillard, E., Meynier, A., de Planhol, X., and Sautter, G.** (1957) *Structures agraires et paysages ruraux*, Nancy. (A fundamental work for every study of rural landscapes.)

Lamour, Philippe (1963) 'L'aménagement du littoral languedocien', *Revue Bas-Rhône—Languedoc*, December.

*****Lavedan, Pierre** (1960) *Les villes françaises*, Paris.

Le Lannou, M. (1964) *La France: les régions géographiques*; vol. I, *La France Septentrionale*; vol. II, *La France Méridionale*, Paris.

'Le remembrement rural', *La Documentation Française Illustrée* (1967), Jan., No. 68.

Lebeau, R. (1955) 'Le vie rurale dans les montagnes du Jura méridional'. Thèse, Lyons.

Les grands aménagements régionaux (1967) 1er trimestre, No. 15, Paris.

Livet, Roger (1962) *Habitat rural et structures agraires en Basse Provence*. Thèse, Aix-en-Provence.

Lombard, H. (1951) *Monoculture de la vigne et évolution rurale dans la vallée de la Cèze*, Montpellier.

Lot, F. (1961) *The End of the Ancient World and the Beginnings of the Middle Ages*, New York.

Markovitch, J. J. (1965—66) *L'industrie française de 1789 à 1964*, 4 vols, Paris.

Marres, P. (1950) *La vigne et le vin en France*, Paris, A. Colin.

*****Martonne, Emm. de** (1942) 'La France; Géographie Physique', *Géographie Universelle*, Tome VI, Paris.

Mendras, H. (1959) *Sociologie de la campagne française*, Paris.

Merlin, P. (1967) *Les transports parisiens*, Paris.

Merlin, P. (1969) *Les villes nouvelles*, Paris.

Meynier, A. (1966) *Rennes; Notes et études documentaires*, No. 3257, La Documentation Française, Paris.

Meynier, A. (1969) *Les paysages agraires*, Paris.

Monty, G. (1967) 'Mourenx, histoire d'une ville sans passé', *Urbanisme et Commerce*, No. 7.

Nougier, L. R. (1950) *Les civilisations campigniennes en Europe occidentale*, Toulouse.

*****Nougier, L. R.** (1959) *Géographique Humaine Prehistorique*, Paris.

Pechoux, P. Y. and Kayser, B., *et al.* (1966) *Toulouse; Notes et études documentaires*, No. 3262, La Documentation Française, Paris.

Perpillou, A. (1940) 'Le Limousin'. Thèse, Chartres.

Pierrein, Louis (1965) *Marseille et la région marseillaise*, Association pour l'animation de la métropole provençale, Marseille.

*****Pinchemel, Ph.** (1969) *France: a Geographical Survey*, Paris, trans. C. Trollope and A. Hunt, London. (*This is the best book in English of the geography of France, with an excellent bibliography.*)

Rochefort, M. (1970) *Aménager le territoire*, Paris.

Rochette, R. (1964) 'Un exemple d'implantation industrielle dans la vallée du Rhône: l'agglomération de Roussillon', *Revue de géographie Alpine*, No. 2.

Roupnel, G. (1932) *Histoire de la campagne française*, Paris.

Schéma directeur de Paris (1969), Paris.

Schéma directeur de la Région parisienne (1965), Paris.

Schafert, Th. (1934) 'Le déboisement des Alpes du Sud', *Annales de Géographie*.

Soyer, J. (1965) *La conservation de la forme circulaire dans le parcellaire français* (Ronéotypie).

Thibault, André (1967) *Villes et campagnes de l'Oise et de la Somme*, Centre départemental de Documentation Pédogogique de l'Oise.

Tricart, J. (1948–52) *La partie orientale du Bassin de Paris*. Vol. 1: *La genese du Bassin*. Vol. 2: *L'evolution morphologique du quarternaire*. Thèse, Paris.

Vidal du la Blache, P. (1903) *Tableau géographique de la France*, Paris. (Cited by A. Demangeon, op. cit., vol. 2 (1948), 516–17.)

Wagret, P. (1959) *Les Polders*, Paris.

Additional further reading

General works: in French
Armengand, A. (1965) *La population française au XXème siècle*, Paris.

Faucher, D. (1951–52) *La France; Géographie, Tourisme*, 2 tomes, Paris.

Martonne, E. de (1921) *Les régions géographiques de la France*, Paris.

Pinchemel, Ph. (1963) *Le fait urbain en France*, Paris.

General works: in English
Bloch, M. (1966) *French Rural History*, trans. Janet Sandheimer, London.

Monkhouse, F. J. (1959) *A Regional Geography of Western Europe*, London.

Ormsby, H. (1950) *France: a Regional and Economic Geography*, 2nd edn, London.

Regional works
The French school of geography has published numerous and generally excellent theses that deal with all the regions of France, some general, others more specialized with reference to a particular topic such as landforms, population, economic activities, etc. The general studies of Ph. Pinchemel and G. Chabot list nearly all of them. Below are five references which are typical examples of these works:

Brunet, R. (1965) *Les campagnes toulousaines*, Toulouse.

Bonnamour, J. (1965) *Le Morvan. La terre et les hommes*, Paris.

Bastie, J. (1964) op. cit.

Dugrand, R. (1963) *Villes et campagnes du Bas-Languedoc*, Paris.

Dezert, B. (1969) op. cit.

Index

Limon, 41, 50, 60, 62
Limousin, 11, 14—16 *passim*, 18,
    30, 105
  landscape of, 42
  land use in, 50, 53
  settlements in, 55, 57
Loess, 18, 64
Loire R., 8, 14, 15, 18, 71, 86
Loire region, 11, 52, 72
  cities of, 82—3
  historic development in, 21—2,
    24, 27, 28
  land use in, 36, 54, 66
Longwy, 77
Lorient, 76
Lorraine, 24, 29, 50
  industry of, 77, 79, 89
  landscape of, 37, 41, 43, 44
  settlements in, 55, 56—7, 58
Louis XIV, 28, 76, 86
Louis XV, 86
Louis XVI, 85
Lower-Durance, 48, 49
Lower-Rhône, 57, 65, 74, 105,
    108—9
Lozère, 53
Lutetia (Paris), 24, 72, 82, 111
Lyons, 9, 30, 55, 82, 86, 106—8
    passim
  age of, 20
  history and development of,
    23—4, 72, 76, 95
  industrial quarters of, 89

Mâcon, 71
'Magdalenian explosion', 21
Maine, 39
Maquis, 7, 65
Market gardening, 36
Marne R., 17
Marseilles, 30, 55, 76, 86, 108
Mas, 40
Massilia, 71
Maures, 55
Mediterranean climate, 4, 7, 14
Mediterranean landscape, 39—40,
    43
Mediterranean-Midi, 24, 54, 58, 68
  landscape of, 39—40, 44, 48,
    49, 53

Meix, 48
Menton, 47
Metamorphic rocks, 10—11, 12
Métropoles d'équilibre, 101
Metz, 82
Meuliérisation, 15
Meuse, R., 21
Middle Ages, 25—7, 51, 57, 63, 72—4
Midi, *see* Mediterranean-Midi
Midi-Pyrénées, 30
Millevaches Plateau, 52
Ministry of Agriculture, 105
Mistral, 7, 39, 45, 65, 74
'Mobilist' theory, 16, 18
Modern Age, 27—31, 74—6,
    78—80
Moissac, 64, 73
Monasteries, 51, 73
Montady pond, 45
Montauban, 74
Mont des Avaloirs, 4
Montblanc, 4, 10, 12, 17
Montceau-les-Mines, 77
Mont-Dore, 53
Montélimar, 91, 107
Montereau, 82
Montpellier, 52, 86
Mont-Saint-Michel, 18
Moors, 15
Morvan, 18, 50, 51, 55, 68
Mosaic-openfield, 38, 44
Moselle R., 54
Mountain zones, 5—7
Mourenx, 79, 95—6
Mulhouse, 73
Multien, 38

Nancy, 77, 85, 94
Nantes, 14, 72, 82, 84
Napoléon Bonaparte, 76
Nappes, 12
Narbonnais, 24
Narbonne, 72
Naurouze, gate of, 7
National parks, 31, 52, 68
Natural boundaries, 10, 28
'Nebulae', 77
Neolithic, 21
Neo-technical era, 78—80
Neuf-Brisach, 75—6